American **TYPEPLAY**

PIE

American

PBC

Library of Applied Design

An Imprint of

PBC International, Inc.

Steven Heller & Gail Anderson

Designed by
Alexander Isley
Design

Library Of Congress Cataloging–in–Publication Data

Heller, Steven
American typeplay/by Steven Heller & Gail Anderson
p.   cm.
Includes index.
ISBN 0–86636–194–4   (Pbk ISBN 0–86636–324–6)
1. Printing—United States. 2. Type and type-founding—United States. 3. Graphic Arts—United States
I. Anderson, Gail, 1962-. II. Title
Z208.H39 1994   94–5872
686.2'24--dc20   CIP

Color separation by Fine Arts Repro House Co.,Ltd., H.K.
Printing and binding by Toppan Printing Co.(H.K.) Ltd. Hong Kong.

Printed in China

10 9 8 7 6 5 4 3 2 1

To Paul Rand

Introduction
8

Big and Small
14

Cutting Edge
26

Distorted Faces
38

Hand Lettering
44

Handwriting
54

Jumbled Words
64

Mac Lettering
78

Metamorphic
84

The New Classicism 94

New Faces 102

Nostalgia 110

Puns 126

Street Smart 138

Type Faces 148

Type & Image 158

Typewriter Type 172

The Word 178

Appendix 186

Index 189

Intense as any thriller, lusty as any romance, and wanton as any book on this subject can be, this is a book about type and lettering, and wanton is not an overstatement. Today there is definitely wanton disregard for the rules of typography. Yet one's wantonness is another's freedom. One's rules are another's license. So let's say that this is a book about passion; a passionate, often smoldering love affair between graphic designers and letterforms, in parts a veritable Kama Sutra of typography revealing many kinds of typographic love—from the sensual hot metal kiss to the orgasmic distortion of digital fonts.

Other than type there are few issues that so completely consume the graphic designer. Illustration is fun, layout is challenging, but typography is the sine qua non of all graphic design endeavor. Societies and clubs celebrate it, conferences debate it, and publications dissect it. Like politics and art, the world of typography has its zealots on both the right and left.

And although type itself is often neutral few designers are neutral about typographic issues, as this sampling of quotations attests:

"Now we have personal computers...that allows you to distort and manipulate type at your whim without any knowledge of type..." railed Massimo Vignelli in *Print* magazine in 1992. "Now they've got a tool that gives them license to kill. This is the new level of visual pollution."

"...[W]e are not interested in a passive and servile relationship to communication, but [one] that is rigorously engaging," stated Jeffery Keedy in *Emigre* #21.

"As a typographer, you are the servant of the author..." cautioned Rauri McLean in *Typography* (1988), "Your job is to help the author to reach his public. You are not making works of art of your own; you are transmitting, with as much skill...the words of someone else."

"All language is personal and that, to me, justifies very personal typefaces," argued Neville Brody in *Eye* magazine in 1992.

"Personal typography is defective typography," exhorted Jan Tschicold in *The Form of the Book* in 1975.

Vociferous debates over type's form and function like this have raged for decades among typographers. Going back further in time type has also symbolized ideology and dogma. In the fifteenth century the distinction between capitals and uncials, for example, mirrored the separation of social classes, as well as being a revolutionary alteration of the written "voice." During the 1930s, in the early years of the Nazi regime, sans serif letters were condemned as anti-German—"a Jewish invention," asserted the Nazi propaganda minister Dr. Joseph Goebbels—and were temporarily replaced by the awkward, though decidedly Germanic, spiky Fraktur. Type should be viewed as more than a bridge between writing and print or a manifestation of language: it is a cultural signpost by which a variety of social phenomena can be examined.

Type is one of the cornerstones of civilization. Aesthetics that developed during the early Renaissance, when classical Greek and Roman culture (art and architecture) was reappreciated and revived, directly influenced the design of letterforms and the archetypes of beauty. The standards applied to typographic balance and harmony echoed those of the major arts, and extended to the applied arts, too. Classical typefaces represented the highest ideals of Western culture. As a humanist art, typography during the Renaissance was as important as painting and sculpture. The masters were among the most progressive artisans of the day for they developed forms that extended the boundaries of communications. In a preliterate world they brought the written word to life by providing structure. By giving it form—indeed nuance—they preserved the word in a manner that could be appreciated centuries later.

Types that were developed during the sixteenth and seventeenth centuries continue to be the models for most typographic endeavor today. Whether the method is traditional or progressive, typography is based, either through adherence or rejection, on the basic principles developed during this critical time. For some designers the traditional or classical approach is as sacrosanct as any religious doctrine, and as zealously preserved. "Type is rigid and implacable," wrote Frederick W. Goudy in *Typologia* in 1921. With others the past is not an end in

itself but the foundation upon which to build new traditions. "We've had five hundred years of moveable type now we have mutable type," concedes Matthew Carter in *Fine Print on Type* (1990). Rebellion is built upon this foundation, too. Those who believe that the classical approach represents archaic standards—better entombed than perpetuated—also hold that traditional typography is the embodiment of oppressive formality. "Of all the arts and crafts, none more lives in the dirty tepid bath water of the past than does typography," declared British designer Phil Baines in *Typographic Magazine* (1991) who would agree that type, like twentieth-century art, has become an expressionistic endeavor. Owing to its solemn rationality classicism is viewed by today's practitioners as expressionism's apotheosis.

And yet the Modern movement of the 1920s, though a rebellious one, actually reconciled contemporary and classical values by rejecting timeworn verities in favor of timeless utility. Styleless functionalism was the hallmark of Bauhaus typography, although it eventually evolved into a style. The real tension in typography has for decades existed between rationalism and expressionism, or rather objective versus subjective aesthetics. Jan Tschicold, who having helped codify the objectivist New Typography in 1925 eventually returned to traditional methods, wrote in *The Form of the Book:* "The aim of typography must not be expression, least of all self-expression.... In a masterpiece of typography, the artist's signature has been eliminated. What some may praise as personal styles are in reality small and empty peculiarities, frequently damaging, that masquerade as innovations." Yet despite this admonition, Tschicold was the chief proselytizer for a

movement that attacked the visual redundancy that was the by-product of traditionalism. His doctrine of asymmetry literally stood type on its ear in an effort to garner greater attention. His predilection for sans serif as opposed to serif faces was based on what he and other Modernists believed were objective truths. Yet critics accused them of perpetrating myths to support their assertions of legibility. Perhaps the contemporary Dutch typographer Gerard Unger is correct when in *Emigre #23* he argued, "Tschicold's preference for sans serifs, and his opinion that they...were more legible than typefaces with serifs, were based upon emotional considerations."

Tschicold and other seminal Modern typographers developed the rules of rationalism that were fervently adopted in the postwar era by a new generation of Moderns in Switzerland, Germany, and America that rallied under the banner *Neue Grafik* or New Graphics. They pushed objectivity and rationalism to a precipice where it balanced between being progressive and progressively redundant. In part, this approach developed as a predictable reaction to the fundamentally crass commercial art in which typographic "expression" was characterized by letters frozen in icicles, consumed in flames, and carved with motion-lines to represent, respectively, cold, heat, and speed. Modern typographic principles were developed to prevent the callous abuse of both au courant and passé typefaces and letters. But under the hard rules established to prevent various aesthetic indiscretions, other crimes and misdemeanors were committed. The worst of which was that graphic design, regardless of subject or context, began to look the same. "Oh, Tschicold...under the disguise of neutrality and readability..., your

9

imitators conquered the world," reads the purple prose of Frank Heine in *Emigre #23*. "See what they did to mankind? They hushed it with boredom until its discernment completely slacked. Your imitators suffocated the world with their mediocrity, coated her with global conformity."

It was this trend toward Modern redundancy that led to mediocrity and fostered another movement of aesthetic values that was neither traditional nor Modern, but eclectic. Eclecticism was based on revivals of old-fashioned popular graphic styles such as Victorian, Art Nouveau, and Art Deco. In a prefiguration of Post-Modernism, eclecticism rejected both cold objectivity and elegant classicism in favor of what in today's argot is called the vernacular, the indigenous language of commercial art. The American Moderns, including Paul Rand, Alvin Lustig, and Lester Beall, sought to distinguish themselves from the majority of anonymous commercial artists by taking on the new (and somewhat heroic) titles of "designer for industry" and "graphic designer," and adopted many of the principles of fine Modern art, which underscored a wished for transcendency of the cultural significance of Modern design. The eclecticists, on the other hand, including Push Pin Studios and Herb Lubalin, derived their styles (and strength) from the legacy of *commercial* art, borrowing and appropriating it as personal style.

For the eclecticists universality was rejected in favor of individualism. The Moderns sought a common language, the eclecticists strived for uncommon solutions. The Moderns rejected supercilious ornamentation, the eclecticists enthusiastically embraced it, not in a nostalgic sense but to enhance presentation of the message by warming and personalizing it. Their work was influenced by the past but was decidedly contemporary. The Moderns believed that design should be "of its time"; the eclecticists decided that their times demanded variety, and that revived forms had as much validity as new ones. Moreover, since new phototypesetting technologies were making it possible to achieve unprecedented results, there was an increased potential for typographic expression using both new and old typefaces.

Herb Lubalin, a devout typophile, and in the 1960s a master of commercial typographic "experimentation," argued for change in this way in *Typography U.S.A.* (1959): "We've been conditioned to read the way Gutenberg set his type, and for 500 years people have been reading widely-spaced words on horizontal lines Gutenberg spaced far apart....We read words, not characters, and pushing letters closer or tightening space between lines doesn't destroy legibility; it merely changes reading habits." Lubalin built upon the ideas of earlier twentieth-century type/image-makers, such as Kurt Schwitters and Lazar El Lizzitsky, and blurred the distinction between type and image. In fact, Lubalin's approach was very much of its time given his understanding of the effect of new technologies on contemporary perception. In 1959 Lubalin argued before an assembly of typographers that television had begun to have an impact on the way that type was read, and likened this kineticism to the speed in which type shoots by on advertising on the sides of buses. He reasoned that in this environment smashing letterforms together (which was Lubalin's trademark) and including images in a rebus-like manner made type easier to decipher.

In the late 1940s a pioneer of American typography, Bradbury Thompson, edited and designed the influential periodical *Westvaco Inspirations* in which he encouraged designers to occasionally release type from its moorings and play with it as if it were a toy. His idea, inspired by the Futurists, Dadaists and Surrealists of the 1920s, was that smart typographic puns could be made from letterforms which would enhance reading by providing an additional level of meaning. Thompson made puns with letterforms that released specific sounds, not unlike the onomatopoeic type poems of the Italian Futurists. A decade or so later Herb Lubalin took the idea even further by combining photographs and drawings with expressive letters that underscored or amplified the meaning of a headline. This was serious typeplay—and Lubalin was a fiddler par excellence. Yet his mission was not to toy with or confuse the reader but to promote clarity. "Typography must be clear communication in its most vivid form," warned Bauhaus type master Laszlo Moholy-Nagy. And although Lubalin's display compositions were not of the style that Moholy was promoting, they were indeed vivid, if at times risqué. Despite the liberties that Lubalin routinely took with typography his work was not difficult to decipher. While he tampered with the form, he stayed loyal to the purpose of type which meant that on some level it must be legible.

Legibility, as opposed to quality, is at the heart of the arguments, pro and con, about typeplay and experimentation. "Legibility is a dangerous—and interesting—word," wrote the English type historian Rauri McLean in *Typography* (1988). "It is dangerous because it is so often used as if it had a definitive or absolute meaning. Which it does not have. It is a personal word, neither scientific nor precise."

Therefore, what is illegible to one can be legible to another, depending on one's specific orientation. In the late 1960s, at the same time that Lubalin was tweaking typographic conventions, a younger generation of American *graphistes*, the Psychedelic poster artists, were violently upsetting typographic propriety, and like some of the mind-enhancing drugs that they consumed their unvarnished type compositions were testing the limits of perception. Victor Moscoso, a leading proponent, turned many canonical rules of legibility and clarity upside down. He used vibrating colors and slab serif types packed tightly together in compositions that were as difficult to read as possible. Yet they were not illegible. "The common wisdom that a passerby had to absorb a poster in ten seconds flat was as ridiculous as it was arbitrary; I wanted them to spend five, ten, even fifteen minutes with it," explained Moscoso years later. And why not? The decree that posters had to be simplistic was imposed by advertising experts who believed that in the highly competitive commercial marketplace simplicity provided the competing edge. Moscoso reasoned that the "consumers" of San Francisco rock and roll were not like the typical dashing commuter and could therefore afford the time to absorb and decipher the poster's message. The fact that it was a kind of game that the reader could understand by being a member of the "tribe" made it additionally appealing. Hence, what appeared illegible to the outsider was crystal clear to the cognoscenti.

"Legibility, in practice, amounts simply to what one is accustomed to," wrote Eric Gill in *An Essay on Typography* (1934). And what one was accustomed to in the late 1960s and early 1970s was the loosening of the verbal and visual language. If typography is, as Jan Tschicold once observed, "a servant and nothing more," then it stood to reason that typography would have to reflect the emerging cultural revolutions either in substance or style. In the early seventies, with the demise of psychedelia, graphic design entered a period of uncertain transition from Modern to Post-Modern. As Herb Lubalin had predicted over a decade before, television and video were having a profound impact on perception, and gradually the computer was also beginning to suggest new typographic directions, if only tangentially at first. These factors partly contributed to the inevitable schism of old and new that had its first major eruption in Basel, Switzerland, the home of Neue Grafik and the International Style of rational typography. "Pure typography is not the only way to convey a message," said Wolfgang Weingart, the major proponent and teacher of the new New Typography. "It's value and potential depends directly on its ambiguity."

As a onetime student of the rigid, and anything but ambiguous, Swiss style, Weingart was poised to break the rules of simplicity and clarity. While continuing to use the fundamental elements of Swiss typography—Univers, Helvetica, and Akidenz Grotesk typefaces—he began to deconstruct typographic composition. Complex layers of boldface, italic, and roman letterforms, often set against ambiguous or "noisy" backgrounds, sometimes in what appeared to be an approximation of video display screens, became the paradigm for a new typographic direction and style. In the fast-paced information age, it was reasoned that traditional reading habits—specifically regarding ephemeral materials such as posters, magazines, and newspapers— would eventually be altered by technology, as they have been throughout the history of mass communications. Contemporary typography, the servant of language, needed to include many entry (and exit) points designed for the increasingly more harried reader. Through highlighted and underscored words and phrases, through intersecting ideas and thoughts, this new typography allowed the reader to choose points of interest, much in the way pull-quotes or blurbs had been used in magazines and newspapers. While on the surface this looked like type as texture— ornament, not words—the new method was very much about accentuating the word and stimulating comprehension through the introduction of "type bites." The new Swiss typography began as a youthful rejection of Modern verities yet its multilayered aesthetic eventually became a metaphor for the information and computer ages and was adopted outside the confines of the hothouse. In so doing it posed a threat to the established Modern order, and was dubbed ugly by those whose fundamental beliefs in typographic objectivity were challenged.

"As typography addresses everyone, it leaves no room for revolutionary change," wrote Jan Tschicold in *Print* magazine (1959) in words that spoke for traditionalists and orthodox Moderns alike. "We cannot even fundamentally change one single letterform without destroying the typeset representation of our language and render it useless." But this sermon ignores the fact that global politics and culture were radically altered after World War II, indeed language itself had profoundly changed over that time, and type as its servant also had to undergo periodic overhauls. By the 1980s the social as well as technological environment had been so profoundly changed that all segments of the culture demanded reevaluation. "Lately we've moved into an era of more cultural fragmentation and ethnic celebration...," stated Katherine McCoy in *Emigre* #19, "You have to be a chameleon to shape your message to the audience so that you can resonate with that audience." McCoy, who codirects the graduate design program at Cranbrook Academy of Art, is a proponent of Post-Modern—or what some call deconstructive—typography, a logical evolutionary offshoot of the Swiss grid-busting school, and the most radically experimental manifestations of contemporary American typeplay. What began in Switzerland as a mildly expressive use of letterforms spread to other parts of Europe (notably Holland) and the United States where in academies like Cranbrook, Rhode Island School of Design, and California Institute of the Arts expressionism became an end in itself. Wed to certain avant-garde linguistic theories and influenced by mass media, "decon" or "PM" typography was not only concerned with busting Modern strictures, but developing codes that would "resonate" with various audiences by drawing them in through multiple levels of visual/verbal data, not unlike computer/video games that push the player through increasingly complex levels of stimuli.

"What is new about Cranbrook's direction is the infusion of meaning into the production of a plethora of objects and graphics that have become mundane and boring," wrote industrial designer Niels Diffrient in *The New Cranbrook Design Discourse* (1990). "It can perhaps be argued that Modernism...also had meaning. And indeed it did, but the meaning most often

was in expressing the materials, function, and process rather than the subtleties of human interaction. This often resulting in a kind of dry neatness, devoid of the essential messiness and ambiguity of the human condition." In contrast to the words "neutrality" and "simplicity," which were mantras of the Moderns, "ambiguity" and "complexity" underscore a contemporary, chaotic ethic and aesthetic and reflect what designers today believe represents the harsh realities of life. "Many people feel it's their role in life to destroy all ambiguity," stated Jeffery Keedy in *Emigre* #16. "I think that ambiguity is life itself and it's what makes life interesting. We too often assume that people are so stupid that they can't deal with ambiguity. I think people live for ambiguity and complexity."

As Modernism was a utopian aesthetic and ethical reaction to the debauched bourgeois societies of pre– and post–World War I Europe, and was initially viewed with contempt by the keepers of the bourgeoisie, so is Post-Modernism a response to the archaic and unresponsive strictures and styles that derived from the Moderns. Historically reaction to a previous generation can be either conservative or radical depending on the tenor of the times. That contemporary typography is raucous and anarchic is a logical repudiation of the cool rationalism that marked the immediate past. But it is also a reprise of early Modern (i.e. Futurist and Dadaist principles), which took art to task for being moribund.

The ideal of "art" has recently been imbued in typography, which prior to now was ostensibly practiced as a craft. Not that typography was ever without its artistic underpinnings, for example "Bodoni created typefaces and typography to impress the eye," wrote type historian Allan Haley in

Typographic Milestones (1992), "His designs were studied efforts to be seen as well as to be read..." But certainly the traditionalists agree that typography is, as the British typographer Stanley Morrison once noted, "essentially utilitarian and only accidentally aesthetic." The personal computer has become a canvas on which type has become the equivalent of paint. Digitization has made it possible for the tutored and untutored to play at will, indeed create art with letterforms. Though following the tradition of concrete poetics and letter collages by the early Moderns, their challenge to academic painting does not apply here. Digital type has simply become a new, and by virtue of is ubiquity, an expedient medium for non- or wanna-be designers. For professional designers, taking on the type designer's role is a more hands-on way to deal with the tools of the trade.

Thanks to the Macintosh, typefaces can now be customized and personalized, and this ability has opened the door to both creative excellence and wanton abuse. Thanks to *Emigre* magazine the application of these types and the experiments of young designers are given a sympathetic showcase. "The reason why we are producing so many typefaces at the moment," states Neville Brody in *Eye* magazine, "is to try to break the mystique of typography. In fact, I think in the future everyone will have their own typeface, which is healthy. With computers that respond to handwriting the digital medium will be personalized." But for some this kind of democracy bodes ill. "I think we have to make a distinction between design and art," Massimo Vignelli cautioned in *Print* magazine, "If you are an artist, you can do anything you want. It's perfectly all right. Design serves a different purpose. If in the process of solving a problem you create a problem, obviously, you didn't design."

Vignelli's statement challenges the entire basis of typeplay. He asserts that the design process has a definite beginning, middle, and end, governed by certain absolutes, the purpose of which is to convey information or ideas. In the current design milieu typography has become another vehicle for expression, to be both indulged and seriously considered. The only way to achieve expressionistic satisfaction is, however, through trial and error, with the errors or "problems" being as important to the creative process as the successes. "I try to work intuitively and to provoke an emotional response from the viewer," explained David Carson, art director of *Ray Gun* in *How* magazine (1992). And Carson's playtime on the computer has resulted in a visual language that communicates directly with a specific constituency in the same way that psychedelia did two decades previous, and for that matter, as Jugenstil (Youth Style) did through its unconventional floriated letterforms almost a century ago. Carson experimented with the quirks and limitations of the Macintosh, its layout and type programs, to find out how limiting or delimiting the new technology could be. He quickly found that it had the power to evoke symbolic connections. "Mentally you cut me, allow my pleasures to pour out onto the pages within, visual ecstasy, bridging subconscious, thoughts become reality, piercing type, chiseled into the page, by minds, not hands, grinding the teeth of reality," wrote a *Ray Gun* reader. "Dear Sirs, your magazine is too hard to read..." wrote another.

As Matthew Carter said, "we now have mutable type," and so perhaps we should accept mutable typographic rules. "Gone are the commercial artist's servant role and the Swiss designer's transparent neutrality...," wrote Katherine McCoy in *Design Quarterly* #148. "Forms are appropriated with a critical awareness of their original meaning and contexts. This new work challenges its audience to slow down and read carefully in a world of fast forward and instant replay..." Yet the Modernist repudiation of the new typeplay is not only based on their fervent adherence to what they believe are immutable laws, but the fact that these laws are the foundation on which graphic design has been transformed from a service into a profession. Before the rules existed anarchy reigned, ad hocism prevailed, and professionalism was a joke. Now with these sacrosanct rules being challenged by serious designers with their own cultural imperatives, as well as artistes and wanna-bes with little understanding, the need to find reconciliation is necessary. "There has to be a balance within the overall complexity between the look of the piece and the actual message that is communicated," wrote Nick Bell in *Emigre* #22. "You don't want the readers to be involved purely in the visual treat, because they will ignore the message." It is this attempt at balancing abandon and constraint that is celebrated in *American Typeplay*.

Contemporary typography is not locked into any one system or ideology, but rather serves different functions that demand different approaches. The examples in *American Typeplay* do not narrowly delineate a single movement, trend, or fashion. Deconstructive, vernacular, neoclassical, and other genres are collected here in an effort to suggest the range of contemporary interest in, and of course passion for, type and typography. This is a record of the commonly uncommon, the conventionally unconventional, and the seriously playful approaches that serve various typographic requirements. While this book does not take any ideological stand, it has a philosophical one: Typeplay is endemic to visual communications. It is fueled by imagination, and imagination requires license. In a diverse culture variety should be encouraged, but standards of quality should somehow govern. License is not limitless. For typeplay not to produce monstrous results the question of what is quality should be paramount. Not all experimentation is good. Not all things new have virtue. It is the nature of typeplay that there will be failures, it is the goal of *American Typeplay* to question, and yet celebrate, the successes.

—Steven Heller

of large and small letterforms—not just in the conventional sense between capitals and lowercase or large caps and small caps—gives a work a certain monumentality, indeed it provides the illusion of more than two dimensions. If one thinks of typefaces as the building blocks of design, then toying with random shifts in size is not unlike the typical child's play. Big and small is at once the most simple and curiously complex of the type-plays. On the one hand trial and error born of instinct is necessary to achieve a satisfying result. On the other, instinct must be honed by experience (and taste). Collaging elements without some semblance of forethought does not insure interesting work. Determining the right balance between objects, images, and letterforms is what distinguishes the skilled designer from the amateur. Understanding how to manipulate big and small is essential to making playful compositions. For if the ingredients are mismeasured even a little bit—if the relationships are either not harmonious enough or too disharmonious—the

resulting design, whether a poster, magazine layout, or book jacket, will be nothing more than a confusing melange of diverse forms. Despite the overarching playful abandon required, for big and small to succeed the designer must possess a keen understanding of the formal qualities of the materials being used.

Playing with scale is one of the first games that one learns as a designer. Differences in scale signal differences in attitude, importance, and character. Understanding the relationships between mass is therefore key to producing graphic excitement. In typography the juxtapositioning

B
I G
& SMALL

Book Jacket
As Long As Nothing Happens
Nothing Will

Art Director
Krystyna Skalski

Designer
Carin Goldberg

Photographer
Benno Friedman

© Grove Press 1990

Book Jacket
Cousins

Designer
Archie Ferguson

Photographer
Michael Horner

© Alfred A. Knopf 1992

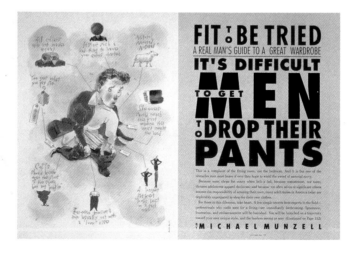

Magazine Spread
San Francisco Focus

Art Director/Designer
Matthew Drace

Illustrator
Barry Blitt

© San Francisco Focus 1990

Brochure
AND Communications

Art Director/Designer
REVERB Lisa Nugent

© *AND Communications* 1991

"an exciting or remarkable experience"

learning

learning can happen wherever you are

The potential for interactive multimedia to reach and teach all kinds of people in all types of environments is quite unprecedented

Even the most prominent members of the education establishment are advocating swift and comprehensive change. Better schools, better teachers, better materials, better results. AND interactive multimedia has a profound impact because it fundamentally restructures the learning experience. Teachers become mentors, students become explorers, and together, they become collaborators in an interdisciplinary that's as engaging as it is enlightening.

ADVENTURE

expedition

safari

trek

"Come my friends,
'Tis not too late to seek
a newer world..."

Epic Poetry   **Ulysses**

Oral History

Mythology

The Art of Storytelling

language

rhythm

pitch

metre

Communication

Allen De Bevoise, *Creative Director*

Morgan Newman, *Architech*

Homer

Black Elk

Alice Walker

Martin Luther King, Jr.

Magazine Spread
The Boston Globe
Supplement

Art Director/Designer
Rena Sokolow

Photographer
Sharon Roberts

© *The Boston Globe
Newspaper Co.* 1993

GRAND GULCH

WHERE YOU CAN TOUCH AN ANCIENT WAY OF LIFE WITH YOUR FINGERTIPS

Brochure
Off-Site Record Management
Art Director/Designer/Illustrator
Earl Gee
© *Earl Gee* 1990

Booklets
Public Eye

Designer
David Cowles

Illustrators
David Cowles
Chris Fisher
Maria Friske
A. Skwish

© *David Cowles* 1992

Robert Hughes

THE HUNDRED-YEAR HISTORY OF MODERN ART—

ITS RISE, ITS DAZZLING ACHIEVEMENT.

T H E   ITS FALL

SHOCK

O F

T H E   N E W

REVISED EDITION

Book Cover
The Shock of the New

Designer
Chip Kidd

© *Chip Kidd* 1990

AIGA/NY American Masters 2

Richard Hess Larger

than Life. Presented by Mark Hess.

With video commentary from Sam Antupit, David Brown,
Lou Dorfsman, Milton Glaser and Miho. November 18 1992, 7-9 pm.
The Katie Murphy Amphitheatre, Fashion Institute of Technology, 227 West 27th
Street, at 7th Avenue, New York, New York.

Members $5, Non members $14. Students info @ $4. AIGA/NY student members and FIT students free.

Many of his peers

believed that he came from the West-
it is part of his myth. But in fact he was
born, in 1934, in Royal Oak, Michigan.
He inherited from his brawling, square-jawed,

Poster
Richard Hess

Designer
Robert Appleton

Photographers
Tom Hollyman *color*
Dmitri Kasterine *b/w*

© *AIGA/NY* 1992

19

[POSTSCRIPT IS THE LINGUA FRANCA OF THE COMPUTER WORLD]

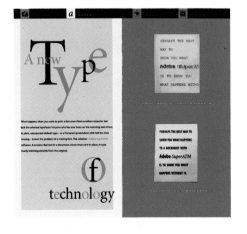

Annual Report
Adobe Systems Incorporated

Creative Directors
Aubrey Balkind
Kent Hunter

Designer
Kin Yuen

Illustrator
Henrik Drescher *above right*

© *Adobe Systems Incorporated* 1993

Book Jacket
Sylvia Plachy's Unguided Tour

Designer
Yolanda Cuomo

Photographer
Sylvia Plachy

© *Aperture Foundation* 1990

Magazine Spread
Rolling Stone

Art Director
Fred Woodward

Designer
Debra Bishop

Letterer
Anita Karl

Photographer
Andrew Eccles

© *Wenner Media, Inc.* 1991

Magazine Spread
Rolling Stone

Art Director
Fred Woodward

Designers
Fred Woodward
Gail Anderson

Illustrator
Al Hirschfeld

© *Wenner Media, Inc.* 1993

Book Jacket
My Hard Bargain

Designer/Photographer
Chip Kidd

© *Chip Kidd* 1989

Book Jacket
Out of Work

Designer
Archie Ferguson

Photographer
Anne Turyn

© *Alfred A. Knopf* 1993

Poster
Big P Little O, Little O Big P

Art Director
Paula Scher

Designers
Ron Louie
Paula Scher

© *Pentagram* 1992

twenty-one

collected stories

Book Cover
Ward Just: 21 Collected Stories

Art Director/Designer
Paula Scher

© *Pentagram* 1990

the next sounds you hear >

VOLUME 1

Promotional CD/Package
The Next Sounds You Hear

Art Director/Designer
Frank Gargiulo

Photographer
Diana Klein

© *Atlantic Recording Corp.* 1993

23

Book Cover
Hats

Designer
Helene Silverman

Photographer
John Dugdale

© *Clarkson Potter* 1991

24

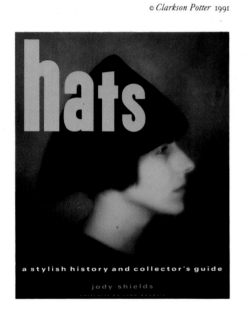

Book Jacket
Squabble

Art Director
Sara Eiseman

Designer
Carin Goldberg

Photographer
Benno Friedman

© *Houghton Mifflin* 1990

Poster
The Big A

Art Director/Designer
Paula Scher

© *Pentagram* 1991

Magazine Spread
San Francisco Focus

Art Director/Designer
Matthew Drace

Letterer
Tim Carroll

© *San Francisco Focus* 1990

The big A.

Chapter 2

Changes in design begin at the edges and cut their way, often on a jagged course, toward the center. In typography, like any other visible visual art, change is accepted timidly at first, then as it gathers momentum the adherents grow in number. The more the new is seen, the less the shock is felt, and with enough followers the edge eventually dulls. History shows that challenges to the typographic canon have been wed to changes in basic form. Given that type is a mediator of language the degree to which change takes place is limited. In recent years as the notion of typographic neutrality has been seriously debated, and the computer has made typographic personality ever more possible, those on the cutting edge have aggressively played with expressionistic approaches. While much of what has been produced is too personal for widespread use, the lessons learned from these experiments have become a foundation for further exploration. The pioneers of expressionistic form have proven that rules of type are not only mutable but often irrelevant. They have also proposed that in addition to being a servant of meaning, typography can invoke its own meaning. Some cutting edge typography is built on the necessary foundation that discovery is a natural order, some is merely the regurgitation of what has been adopted as style. Perhaps only time will tell what work will have legs and what will be artifice. The cutting edge of the past five years has been accused of crimes against qualitative standards, but in the end—whether effective or not the lessons learned from the cutting edge are endemic to the viability of contemporary typography.

CUT-
TING
EDGE

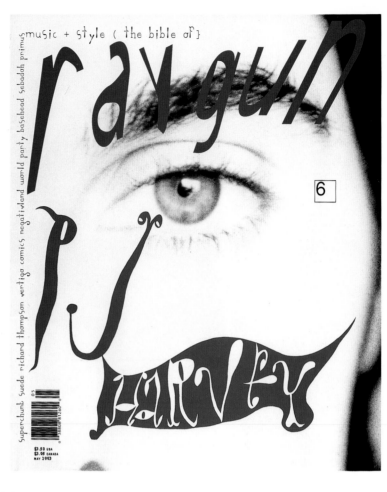

Magazine Cover/Spread
Ray Gun

Designer
David Carson

Hand Letterer
Calef Brown *right*

Photographers
Colin Bell *right*
Skid *below*

© *David Carson Design* 1993

28

Magazine Spread
Beach Culture

Designer
David Carson

© *David Carson Design* 1991

entertaining.

informing.

empowering.

mtv.
involved
in a changing
world.

Media Kit
MTV

Creative Directors
Aubrey Balkind
Kent Hunter

Designers
Andreas Combuchen
Johan Vipper

© *MTV Networks* 1992

>SPECIALS<

only
the biggest **stars.**
only the biggest
events.
only on
MTV.

> Led by the highly rated MTV Video Music Awards, MTV Specials have broken through >
to become some of the biggest events on **the small screen.**

mtv. the
passion is
mutual.

29

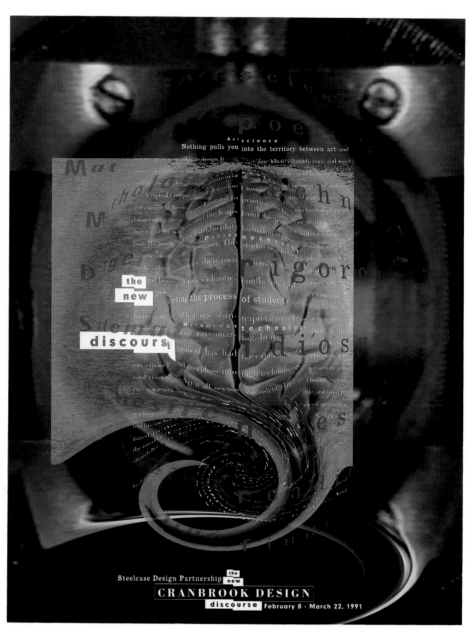

Studio Gift
Smoke Bomb in Bag

Designers
SMOKEBOMB STUDIO
Nancy Mazzei, Brian Kelly

© Smokebomb Studio 1993

Poster
Incite Insight

Designer
Margo Chase

Photographer
Merlyn Rosenberg

© Margo Chase 1992

Poster
Cranbrook Design

Designer
P. Scott Makela

© P. Scott Makela 1989-90

Magazine Spread
Beach Culture

Designer
David Carson

Photographer
Art Brewer

© *David Carson Design* 1991

Record/Cover
Second Hand Rhythm Tool

Designers
SMOKEBOMB STUDIO
Nancy Mazzei, Brian Kelly

© *Smokebomb Records* 1993

Brochure/Poster
Overview of Otis

Designer
REVERB Lisa Nugent

Photographers
Lisa Nugent
Steve Callis

© *Otis College* 1992

Magazine Cover
Design Quarterly

Designer
P. Scott Makela

Design Assistant
Alex Tylevich

© *P. Scott Makela* 1993

Book Cover
Treepeople

Designer
Art Chantry

© *Art Chantry* 1992

Catalog
Art Center College of Design

Creative Director
Stuart I. Frolick

Designer
Rebeca Mendez

Associate Designers
Darren Namaye
Darin Beaman

Photographer
Steven A. Heller

© *Art Center College of Design* 1992

56 Management's Responsibility for the Financial Statements
57 Segment Sales and Income
58 Management's Discussion and Analysis
61 Selected Financial Information
62 Consolidated Balance Sheet
63 Consolidated Statement of Income
64 Consolidated Statement of Stockholders' Equity
65 Consolidated Statement of Cash Flows
66 Notes to Consolidated Financial Statements
66   1.   Summary of Significant Accounting Policies
67   2.   Acquisitions
67   3.   Accounts Receivable
67   4.   Inventories
68   5.   Property, Plant and Equipment, at Cost
68   6.   Investments
68   7.   Intangible and Other Assets
69   8.   Debt
69   9.   Accrued Expenses
70   10.   Stockholders' Equity
71   11.   Research and Development
71   12.   Employee Benefit Plans
73   13.   Leases
73   14.   Other Income (Expense), Net
74   15.   Income Taxes
75   16.   Earnings Per Share
75   17.   Industry Segment and Geographic Area Information
77   18.   Summarized Quarterly Results of Operations (Unaudited)
77   19.   Contingencies
78 Report of Independent Public Accountants

Annual Report
EG&G

Art Director
FRANKFURT BALKIND PARTNERS
Kent Hunter

Creative Directors
FRANKFURT BALKIND PARTNERS
Aubrey Balkind, Kent Hunter

Designers
FRANKFURT BALKIND PARTNERS
Andreas Combuchen, Hans Neubert

© EG&G 1993

34

Brochure
Gilbert Paper

Designer
THIRST

© THIRST 1993

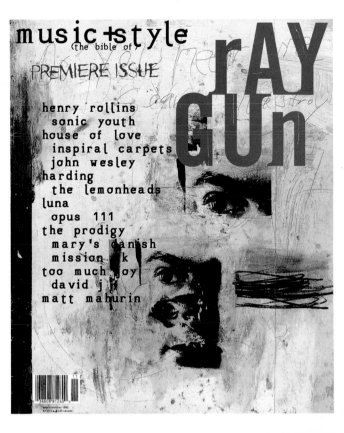

Magazine Cover
Ray Gun

Art Director/Designer
David Carson

Illustrator
Larry Carroll

© *David Carson Design* 1993

Magazine Cover
Ray Gun

Art Director/Designer
David Carson

Photographer
Matt Mahurin

© *David Carson Design* 1993

Poster
Smokebomb Promo #1

Designers
SMOKEBOMB STUDIO
Nancy Mazzei, Brian Kelly

© *Smokebomb Studio* 1992

Book Spread
Rethinking Design: Doing Nothing

Designer
P. Scott Makela

© *P. Scott Makela* 1992-93

End Papers
Facing New York

Designers
Yolanda Cuomo
Naomi Winegrad

© *Bruce Gilden and*
Cornerhouse Publications 1992

Magazine Spread
Emigre

Art Director/Designer
Rudy Vanderlans

© *Emigre* 1992

And so a graphic designer, although one may be antisocial, cannot not be social, cannot

be isolationist. To work as a designer means taking part in the discussion as an individual.

The discussion may be intimate, it may be very public, but most of all, it is an individual speaking with others.

It follows then that to join the discussion or to be conversational, an individual must have a voice. In order to converse effectively—or rather to effectively contribute to a conversation as an individual—the attitude of the voice or her or his' identity needs to be readily apparent.

Designers should take a stand, express a point of view; their work should make

transparent

politics, bias, passions, emotions,

Since a graphic designer "converses" through a printed work, it is especially easy now, with the everyday use of computers in design, to unveil the designer's personal thinking process—by leaving traces and odds and ends of production in the final result. By leaving evidence within the finished product of the physical process (an ironically hand-crafted quality), it is possible for designers to actually represent a discourse. The antithesis of individual representation within graphic design is the corporate logo. In "The Rise and Fall of the Corporate Identity", Ken Garland's argues that the corporate logo cannot represent any one thing or person. In fact, Garland continues, that the most successful and obscene use of the logo was by the Nazi party.

In a lecture delivered at Brunswick in May 1910, he stated: "It is particularly important for Germany, which has now achieved political power, also to win power in artistic areas...In this way, German art and technology will work towards one goal: towards the power of the German nation, which reveals itself in a rich material life ennobled by intellectually refined design." FRIGHTENINGLY WELL DESIGNED So here's our paragon: even at its inception, corporate identity is infused with over-weaning, elitist notions of power and the imposition of order by the visionary few. It is no coincidence, the most effective and arguably the best designed corporate identity of the twentieth century was the one that represented the most effective, arguably the best organized, socio-political system of the twentieth century; nor that it arose in Germany and that it was imbued with Nietzschean concepts of the ÜBERMENSCH. It was also the most obscene of all totalitarian regimes. This tempts the question: Is it only the monolithic, all-powerful organizations like AEG or the Nazi Party which can make really effective use of corporate identity? Certainly, the near-monopoly of AEG gave the company an assurance that was immensely helpful to Behrens in his design program. And the total control exercised by the Nazi regime over its workforce and the availability of resources was equally important to Albert Speer in his impressive devices of corporate identity at great gatherings like the Nuremburg Rallies and in bombastic city planning exercises like the North-South Axis in Berlin, to which, incidentally, Behrens contributed his last architectural work: an office building for AEG) The proposition is also born out by a number of postwar examples of which the corporate identity program for IBM by Eliot Noyes, as design director, and visual and Paul Rand, as design consultant, was—and still is—a model. IBM offers a prime illustration of the contention that, however well designed, a ubiquitous corporate identity is ultimately a calamity just BECAUSE it is ubiquitous. That's the bitter lesson we've only just begun to learn.

"Corporate identity," Garland claims, " is infused with over-weaning, elitist notions of power and the imposition of power by the visionary few. "

Yet in order to represent everything, corporate identities become too diffuse, too bland, too all-encompassing.

When we shower the design periodicals and quality newspapers with angry complaints about the blowsy bugler of BT, we are still missing the point. True, the BT style is an even more footling bit of nonsense than the Prudential popinjay, also from the same design office. But any corporate identity that puts itself about as ostentatiously as these two is offensive, whatever it looks like. NO MORE CASH FOR CANDYFLOSS

So what's to be done? Well, to some extent the problem has solved itself. I cannot believe that any large company will be prepared to fling its money about on candyfloss graphics to spend at all, Assuming, therefore, that they have any money to spend at all, what portion of it can be justifiably channelled in our direction? For starters, we can throw in our lot with those local authorities, civic amenity groups, town planners and others concerned with the depredations of multinational companies, hypermarkets and recently "liberated" public utilities who have been allowed to blazon their insistent company image over our towns and countryside with minimum control from central government. With them, we can promote the idea of the spirit of the place. Not a new idea, of course; it's probably as old as the first human society. It is a vital part of the training and development now that they may not of graphic designers have as much or more influence on the appearance of some environments?

Then we could attempt to persuade the multinationals and other biggies that swanning around the globe about their bigness is increasingly counter-productive.

There's no reason for corporations to employ such monolithic identities. Perhaps corporate identities could be broken down into a system of logos to closer represent different individuals and various facets of a given corporation.

Although "visual babel" illiteracy are being hurled from all sides, at the same time there for designers the demise corporate identity by

Think about it. (I wouldn't be surprised if it hasn't occurred to them already: imagine the embarrassment when we turn up at the board room with our next Corp ID proposals and the hard men frown at it and say, "Bit monolithic, isn't it? Does it have to be quite so ostentatious?") And can we divest ourselves of some of the gruesome hangers-on in our business: the rejects from ad agencies and sales departments who've conned us into thinking that they, rather than we, have their fingers on the pulse of business and industry. Finally, I offer you Garland's Law of Corporate Identity: that the degree of memorability and distinction applicable to any organization should be in inverse ratio to the size of its annual profits or the size of its chief executive's salary, whichever is the greater.

The successful Graphic Designer is, in short, inspired to create—and make every effort to see that his creation reaches out to the viewer with meaning

cultivating individual identities (and peculiarities, "character," personal style) —that is, to be truly conversational in their work.

Magazine Spreads
Emigre

Art Director
Rudy Vanderlans

Designers
Gail Swanlund *above*
Anne Burdick *left*

© *Emigre* 1992

Chapter 3

Before phototypography came of age in the late 1960s there was little attempt at distorting typefaces. Yet the idea of stretching, pulling, and otherwise contorting a headline or text block was not unheard of. Designers working in hot metal interested in exploring this avenue of expression attempted cumbersome processes to do their dirty work. With the widespread introduction of phototypesetting machines in the sixties—notably the Phototypositor—letters could be smashed, overlapped, and otherwise toyed with at will. The availability of anamorphic lenses contributed to, indeed encouraged such play instincts. But what was the reason for distortion? Was it merely vandalism or was there a viable goal? Perhaps both. For some designers distortion was youthful mischief, not unlike scrawling graffiti on a billboard. For others it was rebellion against typographic tradition. With the advent of digital technology distortion became even easier, if not more in demand. While this too suggests a certain amount of mischievousness among young designers, cut with a bit of rebellion, distortion today is a function, indeed a code, of the times. Distortion comes naturally on television and video screens. Where once legibility depended on perceiving the sharp edges of letterforms surrounded by ample negative space, one can now discern word-images in motion. Like military spotters, who are trained to identify planes, ships or cars from their fast-moving silhouettes, readers today are able to derive meaning from kinetic letterforms. People are used to being bombarded with moving words, and therefore can read in spite of the distortion. The deliberate contortion of today's letterforms builds upon this new, shall we say evolutionary, skill. But it is also a means of exploring new realms of perception. Distortion provides new textures against which designers can at once test legibility and create new visual paradigms. Although not a suitable method for all communications, distorted faces can enliven print by extending its boundaries.

DISTORTED FACES

Logo
Bryce Goggin Recording
Designers
SMOKEBOMB STUDIO
Nancy Mazzei, Brian Kelly

© Smokebomb Studio 1992

On-Air Logo
MTV Spring Break
Designers
SMOKEBOMB STUDIO
Nancy Mazzei, Brian Kelly

© Smokebomb Studio 1992

CD Package
Trance Fusion
Designers/Illustrators
SMOKEBOMB STUDIO
Nancy Mazzei, Brian Kelly

© Sonic Records 1993

Record Cover Logo
Whiskey for the Holy Ghost
Designer
Art Chantry

© Art Chantry 1993

Book Jacket
The Ice at the Bottom of
the World
Designer
Chip Kidd
Photographer
Drew Pleak

© Chip Kidd 1989

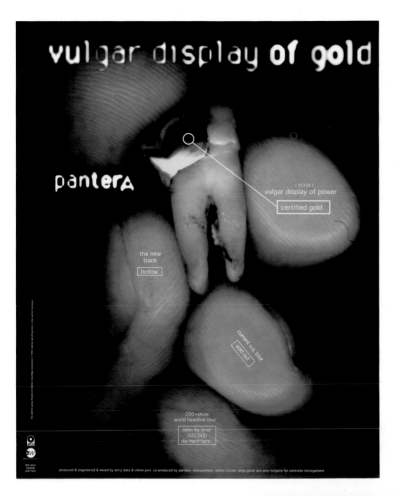

Advertisement
Pantera Gold

Designer/Photographer
Charlie Becker

© *Atlantic Recording Corp.* 1993

CD Package
Time for a Change

Designer
Steve Boyd

© *Bar / None Records, Inc.* 1989

Postcard
Cal Arts

Designer
Somi Kim

© *California Institute of the Arts* 1990

Book Jacket
William Burroughs: A Biography
Designer
Louise Fili
© *Louise Fili* 1993

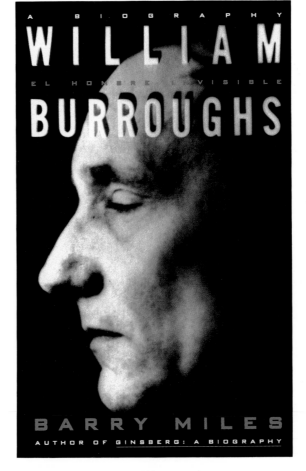

Book Jacket
Bone
Art Director
Victor Weaver
Designer
Carin Goldberg
© *Hyperion Books* 1993

CD/Package
700 Miles
Art Directors
Ria Lewerke
Jackie Murphy
Designer
Sean Smith
Photographer
Josef Komdelka
© *BMG Music* 1993

Poster
Bomb the Pentagon
Designer/Illustrator/Letterer
BLACKDOG Mark Fox
© *Mark Fox/BlackDog* 1991

Logo
Detroit Pistons
Art Director
NBA Tom O'Grady
Designer/Letterer
BLACKDOG Mark Fox
© *Mark Fox/BlackDog* 1992

43

Magazine Spread
Emigre
Art Director/Designer
Rudy Vanderlans
Photographer
THIRST Rick Valicenti
© *Emigre* 1989

Chapter 4

Before movable type the scribe was the principal letterer. Before phototypography the hand letterer, the descendant of the Medieval scribe, was the primary creator of informal letterforms. Hand lettering is an ancient and highly respected ability. In the 1920s and '30s before photostats were prevalent (or cost-efficient) the most skilled typographers rendered even the most standardized display typefaces by hand in arrangements that suited their purposes. For the late Moderns mixing formal faces with sugges-tive hand lettering was a way of adding humor to their work. In the wake of the digital explosion hand lettering has atrophied somewhat, but talented letterers are still in demand to create, indeed invent, forms that are either too difficult for the computer to accomplish or simply where the need is for hand-over mechanical work. Although achieving the perfect hand-lettered piece is not easy—once a style or manner is determined meticulous planning is necessary to get the right result—some examples look as though they instantaneously materialized. Yet for hand lettering to be virtu-ous today, it must look like it was done by hand—a somewhat archaic idea in the digital age. This means that despite the excruciating pain to produce the perfect letterforms, some imper-fection must be noticeable to the tutored, and even untutored eye. On the other side of the coin, hand lettering is also a symbol of defiance against the encroach-ment of technology. In an era when perfect typefaces can be "drawn" on the screen, the unfaltering human hand suggests a mastery of the form. Yet there is a third manifestation for hand lettering in concert with (and reproduced by) computer-aided technology. In the anything-goes design environment the combina-tion of formal and informal letterforms is a means of injecting texture into what otherwise might be one-dimensional work. The hand-lettered form allows the designer to break from the rigid strictures of "pure typography."

46

CD Package
Mr. Wendal
Designer
Randall Martin
Photographer
Keith Ward

© Chrysalis Records,
a division of EMI
Records Group, NA 1992

CD Package
Natural
Designers
Marc Cozza
Randall Martin
Photographer
Sheila Turner

© Chrysalis Records,
a division of EMI
Records Group, NA 1993

Magazine Spread
Rolling Stone
Art Director/Designer
Fred Woodward
Letterer
Anita Karl
Photographer
Albert Watson

© Wenner Media, Inc. 1992

Magazine Cover
New York
Art Director
Syndi Becker
Design Direcor
Robert Best
Designer/Letterer
Anthony Bloch

© Anthony Bloch 1992

Magazine Spread
Rolling Stone

Art Director
Fred Woodward

Designer/Letterer
Gail Anderson

Photographer
David Katzenstein

© *Wenner Media, Inc.* 1990

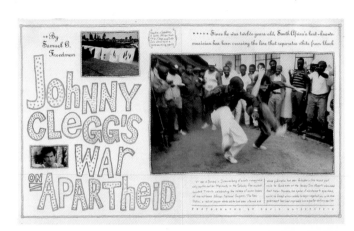

Magazine Page
Rolling Stone

Art Director/Designer
Fred Woodward

Photographer
Bruce Weber

© *Wenner Media, Inc.* 1990

Sales Kit
Plan It for the Planet

Art Director
Julie Wilson

Designer
Michelle Willems

© *Nickelodeon* 1993

Logo
Private Clubs
Designer/Letterer
Bernard Maisner
© *Bernard Maisner* 1990

49

Logo
New York Zoological Society
Designer/Letterer
Bernard Maisner
© *Bernard Maisner* 1991

Lettering for Book Cover
The Many Lives of Elton John
Designer/Illustrator
Bernard Maisner
Publisher
Carol Publishing Group
© *Bernard Maisner* 1992

Logo
Taverna Christina

Designer
Scott Ray

© *Peterson & Company* 1986

Record Logo
The Leon Thomas Blues Band

Designer/Letterer
Bernard Maisner

Record Company
CBS Records

© *Bernard Maisner* 1990

50

Logo
Mark Ryden Illustration

Designer
Mark Ryden

© *Mark Ryden* 1992

Poster
Rosarito-Ensenada Bicycle Ride

Designer/Illustrator
Gerald Bustamante

© *Gerald Bustamante* 1992

Magazine Cover
Rolling Stone

Art Director/Designer
Fred Woodward

Letterer
Laurie Rosenwald

Photographer
Mark Seliger

© *Wenner Media, Inc.* 1991

Poster
U.S.C.

Art Director/Designer
Laurie Rosenwald

Publisher
University of Southern California

© *Rosenwald/U.S.C.* 1992

Poster
Cosmic Thing

Art Director/Designer
Pat Gorman

Letterer
Frank Olinsky

Photographer
Virginia Liberatore

© *Manhattan Design/*

Virginia Liberatore 1989

Magazine Spread
Rolling Stone

Art Director
Fred Woodward

Designer
Debra Bishop

Letterer
Anita Karl

Photographer
Mark Seliger

© *Wenner Media, Inc.* 1990

Logo
Nordstrom Sales Mark

Designer
Art Chantry

© *Art Chantry* 1987

Poster
Moonshake

Art Director
Marko

Designers
SMOKEBOMB STUDIO
Nancy Mazzei, Brian Kelly

© *Matador Records* 1993

Book Jacket
The Lover

Art Director/Designer
Louise Fili

Hand Letterer
Craig de Camps

© *Louise Fili* 1984

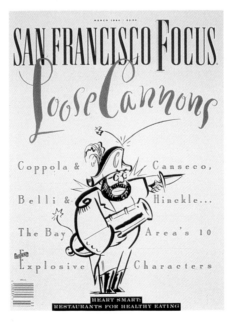

Magazine Cover
San Francisco Focus

Art Director/Designer
Matthew Drace

Illustrator/Letterer
Tim Carroll

© *San Francisco Focus* 1990

Chapter 5

Unlike hand lettering, which even when seemingly informal is based on formal constructs, handwriting is the most casual approach to lettering. Handwriting is to hand lettering or calligraphy what typewriter type is to typeface design. Most everyone has a handwriting style that develops in school from standardized approaches such as the Palmer Method. Like other personal characteristics, handwriting usually evolves consistent with the personality who is using it—and handwriting analysts are quick to point to certain

defining traits that speak volumes about the particular writer's character. As common as it is in everyday life, handwriting is not widely used in graphic design. Perhaps the informality of handwriting suggests a lack of authority. But periodically designers turn to handwriting as a plaything. They test its limits and stretch its boundaries; goose it, contort it, and caress it. In the 1950s, record designer Alex Steinweiss took his signature and developed it into a typeface that was humorously called "Steinweiss Scrawl." While most designers would not have the hubris to develop integrated alphabets from their own writing styles, occasionally a specific problem can be solved this way. In the 1970s numerous record albums and promotions, particularly those for solo recording artists, were adorned with handwriting as if to suggest a personal greeting from the soloist to the audience. Similarly, magazines used handwriting as headlines to indicate a more personal essay than the typical reportage. For some designers

handwriting was fast, cheap, and of course, expressive. Before the digital age many inexpensive alternative publications were replete with handwriting to offset other expenses. Today, however, with the plethora of cheap laser-printed type, using handwriting does not cut many corners. But in the atmosphere of experimentation and play, handwriting is still a way of personalizing graphic design.

Hand
writing

Album Cover
Slanted and Enchanted

Designer
PAVEMENT, INC. Stephen Malkmus

© *Matador Records* 1992

Book Jacket
A Quick Kiss of Redemption
and Other Stories

Art Director
Linda Koserin

Designer
Carin Goldberg

© *William Morrow* 1991

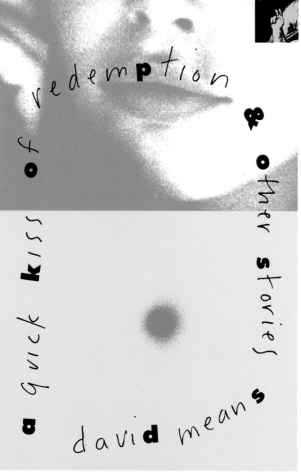

CD/Package
All Jets Are Gonna
Fall Today

Designers
CHOCOLATE USA
Lisa Wagner

© *Bar / None Records, Inc.* 1993

58

Book Jacket
Grey Is the Color of Hope
Designer
Chip Kidd
© *Chip Kidd* 1988

Book Jacket
Pencil Letter
Designer
Chip Kidd
© *Chip Kidd* 1989

Book Jacket
The Cover Artist

Art Directors
Carin Goldberg
Frank Metz

Illustrator/Letterer
Isabelle Derveaux

© *Simon & Schuster* 1991

60

Greeting Card
Big Stars

Designer
Laurie Rosenwald

© *Laurie Rosenwald and
Virgin Records America* 1991

Promotional Brochure
See Jane Print

Art Director/Designer
ROBERT VALENTINE INC.

Illustrator
Jessie Hartland

©*Gilbert Paper* 1993

61

Comic Book Cover/Page
Snake Eyes

Designer
Jonathon Rosen

62

CD Package
Gravity Dance

Art Director
Pat Gorman

Illustrator
Henrik Drescher

© *Manhattan Design/Henrik Drescher* 1990

Postcard
Leo Lionni

Designer/Calligrapher
Robert Appleton

© *AIGA/NY* 1993

CD/Package
With My House

Art Director/Designer
Jean Cronin

Photographer
Lisa Peardon

© *Third Stone/Atlantic
Records* 1993

Chapter 6

In the 1960s smashed and overlapping letters indicated contemporaneity in graphic design. Phototypesetting made it possible for excruciatingly tight settings, which was an exceedingly difficult feat with hot metal. Traditionalists railed that this style was the downfall of typography, while progressives argued that it was merely a playful approach that hadn't been done because the technology was not previously available. In the end it had its proponents and adherents, was popular for a while, yet over time lost its novelty. The same has been said for the Jumbled Word school of typography. The layering, butting, and intersecting of headlines and body texts has been referred to as a pox on typography by the old school, but by the young it has long since transcended fashionable rebellion for status quo. Jumbled word or "rap typography," as one critic has pejoratively called it, is a rather appropriate manifestation in the current milieu. As smashed and overlapping letters symbolized the quick pace of the daily grind in the sixties, rap typography suggests the diverse public conversations in this ever expanding melting pot. While this does not mean that multiculturalism is the wellspring of jumbled words, it is a contributing factor. Actually, linguistic theory borrowed from academe is its primary source. The concept that language can be turned inside out, or deconstructed, to analyze meaning on various levels has given certain designers a motive for research and play. Jumbled words are at once a rejection of the Modern dictum for clean and simple communications, and have become emblematic of the reconfiguration of written language. In fact, in their pure form jumbled words are akin to footnotes, marginalia, or parentheticals, which are integrated into the text. And yet from these roots a mannerism has developed, sometimes good oftimes irrelevant, in which jumbled words have become nothing more or less than texture.

JUMBLED WORDS

Book Spreads
Listen Up: The Lives of
Quincy Jones

Art Director
Helene Silverman

Design Director
FRANKFURT BALKIND PARTNERS
Kent Hunter

Designers
FRANKFURT BALKIND PARTNERS
Rike Sethiadi, Johan Vipper
Thomas Bricker

© *Courtney Sale Ross,*
Quincy Jones 1990

66

CD
Doo-Bop

Designer
Robin Lynch

Photographer
Annie Leibovitz

© *Warner Bros. Records* 1992

Logo
Red Hot Organization

Typeface/Logo Designers
Helene Silverman
Frank Gargiulo

© *Red Hot Organization* 1993

Album Cover
Red Hot and Blue

Art Director
Helene Silverman

Designer
Frank Gargiulo

© *Chrysalis* 1990

Cole Porter was born approximately one hundred years ago in the middle of America. As a student at Yale University, he began writing songs and became determined to be a professional composer. At that time, American music was dominated by the musical theater. Records barely existed and were of poor fidelity, and movies were silent. Composers strove for Broadway success and earned royalties from the side of sheet music in an era when parlor pianos were as popular as televisions and stereos are today. ¶ By the late 1920's Porter emerged as one of the most important voices of a new American generation celebrating the sophisticated pleasures of the modern age. Yet when the Roaring Twenties

came to an end, America was faced with the hardship of the Great Depression and the political turmoil which led to World War II. Porter's personal life was complicated by having to hide his homosexuality to work professionally and, later, from an accident that left him crippled and in great pain for the latter half of his life. In spite of these public and private hardships, Porter's music continued to uplift the public's spirits without ever pandering to the lowest common denominator. ¶ Porter's work celebrates the power of love to provide meaning in a world where little else makes sense. At the same time, Porter avoided the cliches found in most popular songs by

Let's Fall in Love and John Lennon's Stay. Isn't She Lovely and Frank Sinatra's Taking a Chance by the 1950s a Small built Hollywood and Johnny Mathis, began to transform Porter's music from its theatrical context into modern recorded music. However, Rock'n'Roll began to emerge at the same time to replace Porter's intimate and European melodies with African-American beat and direct emotional pleas. In place of Porter, and other great composers like George Gershwin, Duke Ellington, Jerome Kern, Harold Arlen and Irving Berlin, Rock musicians looked to bluesmen like Robert Johnson for inspiration. In contrast, Porter's music seemed too polished. The revolution in pop sophistication he began devolved into cliche and lost touch with the post-war generation's need for more instant and direct forms of gratification. Thirty years later, Rock music, in turn, lost most of its vitality and sense of originality and artists began to look beyond

Rock for exotic and exciting musical ideas. Along these same lines, this album represents an attempt to rediscover and reinterpret classic pop songs of the pre-Rock era in order to help rejuvenate contemporary pop music. ¶ Recently, musicians, as well as visual artists, writers and filmmakers, have begun to sample or remake existing unusual sounds and images rather than create something new in the traditional sense. Although artistic appropriation is an exciting and responsible form of expression, reminding us that the mass media can transform our sense of reality as much as entertain us or make our lives more efficient, it can also reinforce our sense of social observation. Consequently, we should all be aware that the way an artistic technique may assist in focusing attention on the real social issues of our time, wealth and the environment, free speech, human rights and self-determination, the unequal distribution of wealth and the terrible and tragic AIDS epidemic. It is the hope of everyone involved in this project that the performances on this album represent a wide variety of musical styles without diffusing or defusing Porter's powerful themes of romance and social experimentation. ¶ The sad fact is that AIDS changed the face of an entire generation before most of us had heard of HIV, the virus that compro-

mises the human immune system and invariably causes a slow and painful death in those it affects. That is why the artists participating in this album, and those in the related film program and the fashion designs, have come together to limit for a to urge the practice of safer sex in part by using latex condoms, and for removing the stigma that surrounds those who are HIV positive and/or have AIDS. And by affirming the power of love, and above all romance with intelligence, these artists have appropriated Porter's songs to provide a wonderful series of performances that allow Porter's work, virtually for the first time in the Rock era, not only because it helps to reinvigorate contemporary pop music, but because it seems so opposed to be reminded of in these difficult times, reaffirming the AIDS crisis in order to reinstate unworkable and inflexible conservative morals. But with our support we can win the right to love

and live on their own terms, upholding the responsibilities and the freedoms of the global society we all share. —John Carlin

Poster/Brochure
Image as Weapon
Designer
P. Scott Makela

© *P. Scott Makela/WAC* 1992

Manual
The Knoll Group Identity Guidelines
Designer
CHERMAYEFF & GEISMAR, INC.
Cathy Schaefer

© *The Knoll Group* 1993

Magazine Spread
Rolling Stone

Art Director
Fred Woodward

Designers
Fred Woodward
Gail Anderson

Photographer
Mark Seliger

© *Wenner Media, Inc.* 1993

Book Jacket
The Rolling Stone
Illustrated History of Rock & Roll

Art Director/Designer
Fred Woodward

© *Random House, Inc.* 1992

Magazine Pages
Step by Step

Designers
Rick Valicenti
Gib Marquardt

Photographer
Tony Klassen

© *THIRST* 1990

We believe passionately in the power of print

Brochure
Time Inc., Magazines

Creative Directors
FRANKFURT BALKIND PARTNERS
Danny Abelson, Kent Hunter

Designer
FRANKFURT BALKIND PARTNERS
Kin Yuen

© *Time Inc., Magazines* 1991

Logo
Montage

Designer
REVERB Somi Kim

© *Independent Feature Project/West* 1990

Book Jacket
Trick or Treat

Art Director
Alexander Isley

Designer
Kay Schuckhart

Publisher
Clarkson Potter

© *Emily Gwathmey and Suzanne Slesin* 1992

Brochure
Reading and the Arts of the Book

Designer
REVERB Lisa Nugent

Photographer
Steve Callis

© *The Getty Center for Art and the Humanities* 1992

Poster
Strategic Graphics Inc.
Designer
Robert Appleton
© *Strategic Graphics Inc.* 1992

Logo
Stark/Raving Theatre
Designer
Art Chantry
© *Art Chantry* 1992

Record Sleeve
Birdhouse in Your Soul
Designer
Helene Silverman
© *They Might Be Giants* 1990

The whole city is on fire **VERSE FOUR**
And now it's down to the wire
Time ta call for a National Emergency
'Cause white folk are goin up in smoke
Too fast they ass is out before you know it
So when I light this cocktail cube
Throw it and make sure that it reach:

Yeah mothafucka,
that's for Howard Beach
and Brother Oliver X

So whats next with yall punk-ass cowards
Each of us bring four devils

And lets get this over wit' Yeah no shit
We ain't worried about dyin'...
I think we better give up (Man)...", Naw I ain't even tryin'
I'd rather go out Fightin',
But let yall tell it...
"I'm incitin' the Watts Riot!

THE STERE O TYPE

Verse One

They say a nega-ain't good for nuthin' but a show, talkin' singing and walkin' with a radio, drippin' sweat on the basketball courts, dealinatin', but that's all Sports... or investin' some new kind'a hunchbacks, ta get they picture on a buck'a pancake mix, so I kicks some Hip-Hop, and go to church Sunday ta hit me a Flip-flop... but prayin' ain't all we do, too most we play Bingo and Bar-B-Que; Then days I could praise the lord and still gamble, and eat me'dead-meat then little Black Sambo, but gotta hear sum old ladies, camblin' the holy ghost-ment in they' 80's, and I don't wanna hear no yellin', Naw I'm'a just kick it- and finish this watermelon (Cause I'm the Stereotype)

STILL GOT LUV 4 'UM

CD Package
Kam, Neva Again

Art Director
Richard Bates

Designer
S. Sung Lee

Illustrator
Mac James

Photographer
Todd Gray

© *Atlantic Recording Corp.* 1993

Album Cover
One Hell Soundwich

Art Director
Helene Silverman

Designer
Frank Gargiulo

Illustrators
Gary Panter
Jay Cotton

© *Blast First Records* 1990

Stationery
Morphosis

Designers
REVERB
Andrea Fella, Lorraine Wild
MORPHOSIS Thom Mayne

© *Morphosis* 1993

Magazine Page
Vibe

Designers
Richard Baker
Lee Ellen Fanning

© *Vibe* 1993

Poster/Insert
Emigre

Designer
P. Scott Makela

© *P. Scott Makela/Emigre* 1992

CD Package
Love Me the Right Way

Art Director
Jackie Murphy

Designer
Sean Smith

© *RCA Records* 1993

When Gutenberg invented movable type the letterforms he used replicated Germanic scripts. Although his Mainz press would ultimately open the door for additional styles of type to be developed, his greatest contribution was ostensibly to the technology of printing. Similarly, when Apple Inc. introduced the Macintosh computer its creators never dreamed that it would have such a tremendous impact on graphic design, no less typography. The earliest Macs did not have enough memory to create and store designed layouts. These machines were loaded with default, low resolution bitmapped typefaces that could not compare in quality with existing types. Therefore it took real imagination to understand their potential as a design tool. Within a short time high resolution fonts were put into use, and now thousands are available. But in the interim only a few pioneers attempted to use the roughly hewn faces. Yet thanks to these intrepid souls the Mac became a fount of typographic ingenuity. Making the Mac's limitation into an advantage required a fair amount of play. The machine was more than a serious toy. Making radical bitmapping from the proverbial sow's ear into a silk purse was not easy. But the Mac users determined that smoothing the textures out was not necessarily advantageous, and therefore making silk was not the objective. Nor was Mac lettering a diamond in the rough, but it was the first step in developing typographic norms for the computer. Moreover, Mac type was the basis of a distinct typographic dialect that not only signaled the advent of the age of computer-aided design but of a period of accelerated typeplay. *Emigre* was the clarion of Mac lettering, and in its earliest incarnation as a culture tabloid on the cusp of becoming an influential design magazine it proved the viable application of bitmapped exaggeration. With so many improvements in the technology, today Mac lettering is less of a statement and more of a style, but that it initially provided designers with usable options cannot be undervalued.

CD/Package
Hard Hip Hop
Designer/Type
Elliott Earls

© *Elektra Entertainment* 1993

BAD LETTERING

I HAVE FOUND, IS USUALLY BEGINS WITH THE PREMISE THAT ALL LETTER PREDICTABLE. WIDTHS, LIKE ALL MEN, ARE CREATED EQUAL. THE LAY LETTERER THEN ADDS THE TYPICAL MISTAKES SERIFS TO THE "I" SO IT WILL FILL UP ITS MADE BY LAY LETTERERS SLOT. THERE IS NO CONSISTENCY TO OFTEN FOLLOW SIMILAR THE RADIUSES OF CURVES IN CURVED LINES. I'VE MARVELLED CHARACTERS, NOT EVEN WITHIN THE OVER THIS FOR YEARS. SUCH SAME CHARACTER. MOST OBSERVATIONS FORMED THE PERPLEXING, IS THAT THE BASIS OF A REALLY LOUSEY LAY LETTERER MIXES THICK+ FONT CALLED THIN STROKES WITH MONO-WEIGHT LETTER FORMS. THEN HE CONFUSES THE ORDER OF THE THICK + THIN BADTYP. STROKES OF ROMAN TYPE AS THOUGH HE'D NEVER SEEN A NEWSPAPER IN HIS LIFE OR CAN'T REFER TO ONE.

Set in Cabarga BADTYP

Set in Cabarga CYMBAL. 1234567890

Font Specimen
Cabarga BADTYP
Designer
Leslie Cabarga
*© Leslie Cabarga and
The Font Bureau* 1993

Logo
Rocky River School District
Designer/Letterer
Nancy Bero Petro

Egiziano Classic Black

ABCDEFG
HIJKLMN
OPQRSTU
VWXYZ(&
.,"'‘‘”’?!/-*#)
abcdefghij
klmnopqrs
tuvwxyz12
34567890

Set at 40 point, minus leaded 2 points

Egiziano Classic Black Shadow

ABCDEFG
HIJKLMN
OPQRSTU
VWXYZ(&
.,"'‘‘”’?!/-*#)
abcdefghij
klmnopqrs
tuvwxyz12
34567890

Set at 40 point, minus leaded 2 points

Franklin Gothic Triple Condensed

ABCDEFGHIJKLMN
OPQRSTUVWXYZ(&
.,"'‘‘”’?!/-*#)abcd
efghijklmnopqrstu
vwxyz1234567890

Set at 40 point, minus leaded 2 points. An original design

Franklin Gothic Wide

ABCDEFG
HIJKLMN
OPQRSTU
VWXYZ(&
.,"'‘‘”’?!/-*#)
abcdefghij
klmnopqrs
tuvwxyz12
34567890

Set at 40 point, minus leaded 2 points.

Font Catalog
A Great Collection
Designer
Dennis Ortiz-Lopez

© *Dennis Ortiz-Lopez* 1990-93

O-L Hebrew Graphic Script with Nikkud

Designed for use in Adobe Illustrator without the hebrew finder, this font features a complete set of vowels, hard and soft consonants and hebraic sorts

THIS FONT MAY ALSO BE ORDERED FROM FONTHAUS WITHOUT TECHNICAL SUPPORT

O-L Hebrew Deco

A four-layered titling font designed for use in Adobe Illustrator without the hebrew finder. Consonants only

GOOD LETTERING requires as much skill as good painting or good sculpture.

Although it serves a definite purpose and not necessarily eternity, good lettering

is equal to the fine arts. The designer of letters, whether he be a sign painter, a

graphic artist or in the service of a type foundry, participates just as creatively

in shaping the style of his time as the architect or poet. – JAN TSCHICHOLD

Font Specimen
S.I. Gothic

Designer
Jonathan Hoefler

© *The Hoefler Type Foundry* 1991

Font Specimen
Egiziano Classic

Designer
Jonathan Hoefler

© *The Hoefler Type Foundry* 1991

BEHOLD
SIX EXCITING NEW
FACES
DEVELOPED ESPECIALLY
FOR SPORTS
ILLUSTRATED

S. I. FEATHERWEIGHT

S. I. LIGHTWEIGHT

S. I. HEAVYWEIGHT

S. I. MIDDLEWEIGHT

S. I. WELTERWEIGHT

S. I. BANTAMWEIGHT

KLMNOPQR
ABCDEFGHIJ
GRAZIA BODONI
RSTUVWXYZ
1234567890

Font Specimen
Grazia Bodoni

Designer
Jonathan Hoefler

© *The Hoefler Type Foundry* 1991

83

N ot unlike a visual pun, which is an image that has two or more meanings, the metamorphosis of type and letters is the transformation of a conventional form into another object or image. Graphic design puns are most commonly achieved through the metamorphosis of a letterform into something that is other than its original form, while at the same time it still reads as the letterform. Using hot metal typecase letters the Russian Constructivists arduously transformed letters into human figurations by carefully jumbling the letters so that they still read as a word but also revealed a pictograph or character. In his book of *Calligrames*, the French Surrealist poet Apollinaire metamorphosed words in a poem about rain into the rain itself by composing them vertically down the page, not unlike the naive manner of a child when toying with writing at an early developmental stage. In a prefiguration of Surrealism, the English writer Lewis Carroll in *Through the Looking-Glass* metamorphosed a piece of type into the shape of a mouse's tail to allow the reader the added experience of seeing as well as reading (and hearing) his fantastic tale. Of all the tools for play at the designer's disposal the metamorphosis of type is one of the most difficult, for the result could easily be two-thirds of a pun, as one used to say in elementary school, if it is not smartly done. Yet when successful, metamorphosed type is also one of the most satisfying because it is the quintessential designer's game. The joy derived from realizing and solving the metamorphic puzzle adds greatly to the reader/viewer experience. Which, incidentally, addresses the paramount issue in graphic design—to grab and hold attention.

META
MO
MORPHIC
PHIC

Book Jacket
Lust
Art Director
Sara Eiseman
Designer
Carin Goldberg
© *Houghton Mifflin* 1988

HEAT
WAVE

Logo
Bloomingdale's Summer
Campaign
Creative Director
John Jay
Designer/Typography
Tim Girvin
© *Tim Girvin Design, Inc.* 1985

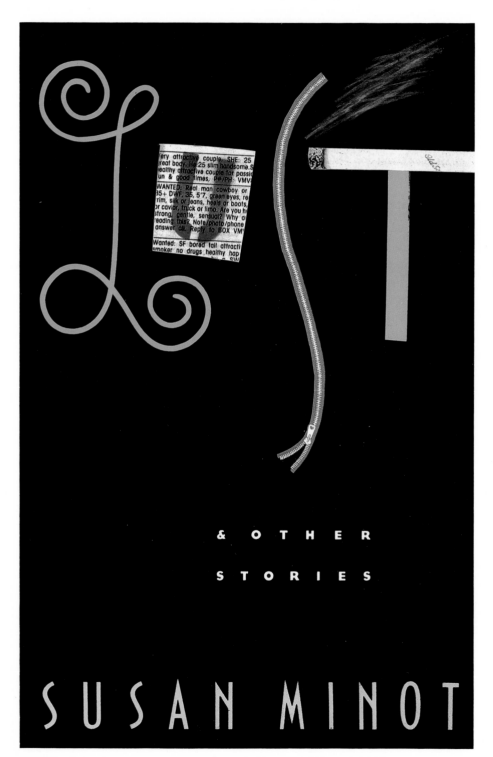

LUST

& OTHER

STORIES

SUSAN MINOT

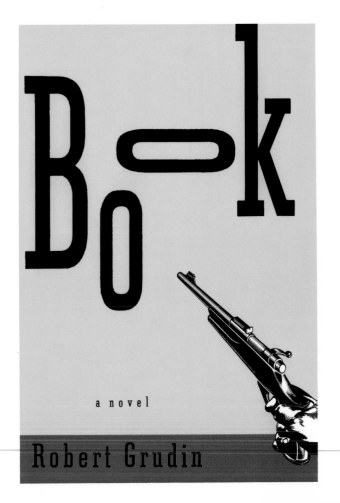

Book Jacket
Book

Designer
Archie Ferguson

Illustrator
Mark Falls

© *Random House, Inc.* 1992

Logotype
Sun Microsystems

Art Director/Designer
Earl Gee

© *Earl Gee Design* 1991

CHIC-*ism*

Poster
Chic-ism

Art Directors
Robin Lynch
Jeff Gold

Designer
Robin Lynch

Photographer
Stephan Sednaoui

© *Warner Bros. Records* 1992

Newspaper Pages
The New York Times

Art Director
Mirko Ilic

Designers
Sam Reep *left*
Gary Cosimini *right*

Illustrators
Milan Trenc *left*

© *The New York Times* 1992

Newspaper Pages
The New York Times

Art Director
Mirko Ilic

Designers
Mirko Ilic *left*
Sam Reep *right*

Illustrators
Alejandro Arce *left*
Ruth Marten *right*

© *The New York Times* 1992

Poster
Design Renaissance

Art Director
Paula Scher

Designers
Ron Louie
Paula Scher

© *Pentagram* 1993

Book Cover
Real Estate

Designer
Paula Scher

© *Simon & Schuster* 1988

Poster
Dallas Art Directors Club

Art Director/Designer
Paula Scher

© *Pentagram* 1992

Movie Logo
Rites of Summer

Designer
FRANKFURT GIPS BALKIND
Peter Nguyen

© *Peter Nguyen* 1988

Logo
Daven Film & Video

Designer
Earl Gee

© *Earl Gee Design* 1991

Poster
SPD Call for Entries

Art Director
Fred Woodward

Designers
Fred Woodward
Gail Anderson

Illustrators
Terry Allen
Dennis Ortiz-Lopez

© *Society of Publication Designers* 1990

GEEK LOVE

A NOVEL

KATHERINE DUNN

BIG SHOTS

Movie Logo
Big Shots
Designer
FRANKFURT GIPS BALKIND
Peter Nguyen
© *Peter Nguyen* 1987

Book Jacket
Geek Love
Designer
Chip Kidd
© *Chip Kidd* 1989

Self-Promotional Piece
Bon Appetit!

Designers
Bernard Maisner
Nora Scarlett

Letterer
Bernard Maisner

Photographer
Nora Scarlett

© *Maisner & Scarlett* 1992

Newspaper Page
The Wall Street Journal

Art Director/Designer
Greg Leeds

Illustrator
David Suter

© *Dow Jones & Co., Inc.* 1990

Chapter 9

From out of the foam of the current wave of complexity comes a new approach to old typography. As a response, indeed a reaction, to the chaotic activity that has come to signify contemporary typeplay, the reappreciation of simple classical methods is gaining new adherents. The New Classicism is not a movement or fashion—by no means is it a new wave—but it does suggest a new sobriety in the wake of what some have criticized as the wanton antics of Post-Modernism. Rather than an ideology based on fundamental strictures, The New Classicism is an alternative form of play. Only this time rather than an experiment with the unknown and untested it is a reconfiguration of the tried and true. And yet this is not a nostalgic approach that desperately recalls the "good ole days," but instead classic types are being reappreciated in decidedly contemporary compositions that derive from, but are not overly influenced by, the latest technologies. The idea that type can be recast in the manner of hot metal has been rejected for the here and now. But that does not mean that typography must be slavishly wed to fashion, either. The New Classicism is being practiced by those who respect the past, but understand the present communications environment. It is also the playing field for those who have seriously toyed with the new wave but ultimately were stymied by the inherent limitations found in its stylistic trappings. The New Classicism is concerned with reducing complexity, focusing on the essentials, and returning to more accessible composition. This implies both a return to the traditional central axis and Modernist ornament-free approaches. But even though the New Classicism is a confluence of these two aesthetics it is not locked into one or the other. The result is often a pleasing, indeed refined, typography that respects the word as meaning (the cornerstone of communication), not as texture.

THE NEW
CLASSICISM

Me

Stories of My Life

Katharine Hepburn

Book Jacket
Me

Designers
Chip Kidd
Carol Devine Carson

© *Alfred A. Knopf* 1991

Book Jacket
White People

Designer
Chip Kidd

© *Alfred A. Knopf* 1990

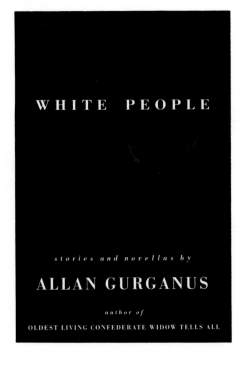

WHITE   PEOPLE

stories and novellas by

ALLAN GURGANUS

author of

OLDEST LIVING CONFEDERATE WIDOW TELLS ALL

BRAHMS

CLARINET QUINTET IN B MINOR, OP. 115

MOZART

CLARINET QUINTET IN B-FLAT MAJOR, K. ANH. 91/516C

SEQUOIA STRING

Q · U · A · R · T · E · T

WITH

MICHELE ZUKOVSKY

C · L · A · R · I · N · E · T

Magazine Spread
Rolling Stone

Art Director/Designer
Fred Woodward

Letterer
Anita Karl

Photographer
Albert Watson

© *Wenner Media, Inc.* 1992

Magazine Spread
Rolling Stone

Art Director/Designer
Fred Woodward

Photographer
Albert Watson

© *Wenner Media, Inc.* 1990

Magazine Spread
Rolling Stone

Art Director
Fred Woodward

Designer
Gail Anderson

Photographer
Matt Mahurin

© *Wenner Media, Inc.* 1993

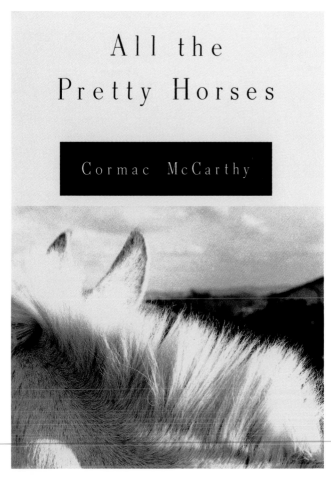

All the Pretty Horses

Cormac McCarthy

Book Jacket
All the Pretty Horses

Designer
Chip Kidd

Photographer
David Katzenstein

© *Chip Kidd* 1992

Book Cover
Genesis and Exodus

Designer
Archie Ferguson

© *Pantheon Books* 1991

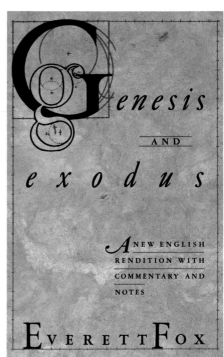

Book Jacket
Ever After

Art Director/Designer
Carol Devine Carson

© *Alfred A. Knopf* 1992

EVER AFTER

GRAHAM SWIFT

Book Jacket
In the Form of a Person

Art Director
Carol Devine Carson

Designer
Barbara de Wilde

Photographer
Paul Schuitema

© *Barbara de Wilde* 1992

in the form of a person ann pyne

Annual Report
Collagen Corporation

Designers
Earl Gee
Fani Chung

Photographer
Geoffrey Nelson

© *Earl Gee Design* 1992

Magazine Page
Rolling Stone

Art Director
Fred Woodward

Designer
Debra Bishop

Letterer
Anita Karl

© *Wenner Media, Inc.* 1992

Book Jacket
A Writer's Life

Designer
Louise Fili

© Louise Fili 1993

Logo
Del Bosque

Designers
Chris Hill
Jeff Davis

© Chris Hill/A Marketing Group 1992

DEL BOSQUE

Book Jacket
The Queen's Throat

Art Director
Frank Metz

Designer
Carin Goldberg

© Simon & Schuster 1993

Chapter 10

The Macintosh has become a tool, if not a platform, for a rash of new typefaces. The word *font*, once used only by printers and graphic designers, has come into common usage. Like other technical words and phrases that have been adopted into the vernacular, *font* will be with us for a long time. Font packages are currently available as common peripherals to anyone who works a PC. The once improbable idea that everyone will own a personal typeface is actually coming

true. If printing was considered a democratic art when only a few people had access to a printing press, and even fewer could run them, what is it now that everyone has access to a PC, laser printer, and even more importantly, type. Like the telephone, the personal computer has become a standard communications medium, and type has emerged as its common voice. It was in the early stages of this environment that timidly at first a few intrepid type designers switched from designing for film over to digital media. Now even designers who would have never thought to call themselves typographers have begun designing customized faces. The availability of type design programs has made it seem that anyone with programmatic skills can achieve the same results as type designers. And while on occasion the neophyte might by chance design a few interesting display letters, the odds of creating a viable alphabet remain slim. The best custom display faces are still those rendered by skilled designers, who have a sense of how the letters will perform in context

and when they converge with other forms. But most important, viable text alphabets must still be administered by those skilled artisans who can wed legibility and aesthetics. The New Faces that are being issued on a regular basis cannot be judged by who designed them (even good designers design bad faces), but the odds are that the most effective are created by skilled designers who understand the nuances of type.

new

FACES

Typeface Specimen
Motion
Designer
Frank Heine
© *Emigre* 1993

Typeface Specimen
Oakland Ten
Designer
Zuzana Licko
© *Emigre* 1986

Typeface Specimen
Missionary
Designer
Miles Newlyn
© *Emigre* 1993

ORIGINAL TYPEFACES
Designed by Barry Deck

Barry Sans Serif
ABCDEFGHIJKLMNOPQRSTUVWXYZ
abcdefghijklmnopqrstuvwxyz
1234567890

Canicopulis Script
ABCDEFGHIJKLMNOPQRSTUVWXYZ
abcdefghijklmnopqrstuvwxyz
1234567890

CAUSTIC BIOMORPH EXTRA BOLD
ABCDEFGHIJKLMNO
PQRSTUVWXYZ
1234567890

Washed Out Plenty
ABCDEFGHIJKLMNOPQRSTUVWXYZ
abcdefghijklmnopqrstuvwxyz
1234567890

PORTFOLIO
TIME & EFFORT CO.

for all your
TYPOGRAPHICAL NEEDS!
call (718)832-5644

Portfolio Page
Original Typefaces
Designer
Barry Deck
© *Barry Deck* 1992

Typeface Specimen
Template Gothic
Designer
Barry Deck
© *Emigre* 1991

Template Gothic

·LIBRIS·
BY JONATHAN MACAGBA

BASED ON THE LETTERING OF AN EARLY
TWELFTH CENTURY SPANISH MANUSCRIPT

AABCCDEFGHH
IJKLMMNOOPPQRS
TUVVWWXYZ&
1234567890LEFI

NOW AVAILABLE FOR THE MACINTOSH OR WINDOWS
TYPE-1 & TRUETYPE VERSIONS INCLUDED

$35 POSTPAID
PA RES. ADD 7%

TO ORDER, CONTACT YOUR DEALER OR ORDER DIRECTLY FROM:
HANDCRAFTEDFONTS CO. ❧ P.O. BOX 14013 ❧ PHILA. PA 19122 ❧ TELEPHONE (215) 634-0634

Font Specimen
Cabarga Kobalt
Cabarga Progressiv

Designer
Leslie Cabarga

© *Kobalt™ Leslie Cabarga*
and The Font Bureau 1993

—F. G. Cooper, c. 1930
"LETTERING
struck an awful snag
in the river of time when printing was invented.
TYPOGRAPHY
tends to establish letterforms
frozen in tradition.
& limited by its mechanical medium."

Set in Cabarga Kobalt

COMPUTER TYPE
blurs the line between hand lettering and type.
In the past, the technical expertise required to
render quality lettering left out all but a few.
The computer has obviated much of the drawing, measuring and inking associated with traditional lettering but it cannot produce correct
letterforms or a feeling for letter design.
The computer-generated wave
which the novice letterer rides to compe-
tence also propels the expert that much farther.

Set in Cabarga PROGRESSIV

HE & SHE

Many writers feel uncomfortable using the masculine pronoun when
referring to a person of either gender. But, recasting a sentence to
eliminate male pronouns is sometimes difficult or undesirable. It may seem
awkward to use both masculine and feminine pronouns (as in "When the
commuter arrives at the station he or she often finds the train late.").
Use of the feminine pronoun alone, as the male is used,
may raise questions in readers' minds as to whether the object of
the sentence is a "she" specifically.
In order to establish a balance of terms when referring to people
generally, when no specific sex is indicated, I have developed a system of
replacement pronouns described below.

She and he become **she** (pronounced suh-he)
His and hers become **hiers** (pronounced hears)
Her and him become **herin** (pronounced hurin)
Man, becomes **man** (pronounced wuh-man)

Now, when a writer speaks of mankind in general the need not worry that
hiers statement will come back to haunt herin.

Set in Cabarga Ojaio Light   Font includes the ligatures ch & ffi

---

Typeface Specimen
Libris Light

Designer
Jonathan Macagba

Foundry
Handcraftedfonts Company

© *Jonathan Macagba* 1993

Font Specimen
He & She Cabarga Ojaio

Designer
Leslie Cabarga

© *Leslie Cabarga* 1993

Font Specimen
Hoefler Text Roman

Designer
Jonathan Hoefler

© *The Hoefler Type Foundry* 1991

Font Specimen
Gestalt

Designer
Jonathan Hoefler

© *The Hoefler Type Foundry* 1991

HOEFLER TEXT ROMAN

72 POINT

Manifestos

48 POINT

Victorian Poster

36 POINT

Enlightened Republic

28 POINT

Wodehouse Story Published

24 POINT

Amalgamated Industries Report

18 POINT

Science provides the modern designer with

14 POINT

When scuba diving off the coral reefs around St. Kitts, he discovered the most remarkable thing. The sunken

12 POINT

Often the Manx deposited itself neatly in front of their Trinitron

10 POINT

The theater's construction was such that it sadly afforded a full view of the show to all but the luckiest patrons

9 POINT

The neighbors all gathered to mourn the passing of dear Agatha, dead at 91 rest her soul, and express their deep concern for the welfare of her old, spacious apartment

7 POINT

Seasoned fishermen are familiar with a variety of shiny lures and the fish they attract. A spinner will often bring bass; pickerel will respond to a black fury fly. The intrepid angler is wont to cast a line with his companions' car keys, for hours of play

CHARACTERS IN COMPLETE FONT

A B C D E F G H I J K L M
N O P Q R S T U V W X Y Z
a b c d e f g h i j k l m n o p q r
s t u v w x y z 1 2 3 4 5 6 7 8 9 0
Á Á À Â Ã Ä å á à â ã ä Ç ç É È
Ê Ë é è ê ë Í Ì Î Ï í ì î ï ı Ñ ñ Ø
Ó Ò Ô Õ Ö ø ó ò ô õ ö Ú Ù Û
Ü ú ù û ü Ÿ ÿ … . , : ; , „ " " ' ' '
^ ´ ` ¯ ˘ ˙ ¨ ˚ ˝ ‹ › « » < > [ ] ( ) { }
/ | \ - – — = ≠ + _ ? ¿ ! ¡ & * ° @ #
% ‰ $ ¢ £ ¥ ƒ © ® ™ ª º - • ¶ §
† ‡ Æ æ Œ œ ß fi fl ff ffi ffl ☞

XAVIER

ABCDEF
GHIJKL
MNOPQ
RSTUV
WXY&Z

AN ORIGINAL
DESIGN BY JASON CASTLE

Font Specimen
Xavier

Designer
Jason Castle

© *Jason Castle* 1992-93

108

ABCDE
FGHIJK
LMNOP
QRSTU
VWXYZ

34

abcdef
ghijklm
nopqrst
uvwxyz
&åçéĝñ

35

109

Typeface Specimen
Bloodstream

Designers
SMOKEBOMB STUDIO
Nancy Mazzei, Brian Kelly

© *Smokebomb Studio* 1993

Font Catalog
A Great Collection

Designer
Dennis Ortiz-Lopez

© *Dennis Ortiz-Lopez* 1990-93

Chapter 11

Nostalgia was once a disease. "Nostalgia, neuralgia, take a bromo and call me in the morning." Actually, in the sixteenth century the nausea and heartburn felt by young soldiers and caused by melancholy and homesickness during wartime was a very serious malady. Today nostalgia, the longing for yesterday, is more a mental (dis)order that affects people who sometimes have never even lived through the particular period that they are nostalgic for. Playing on this passion for the past has made nostalgia, the appropriation of old styles, into a common marketing tool for businesses and their advertising agencies. In graphic design and typography the past has become a viable and ubiquitous plaything. Nostalgia is at best a serious reapplication of historical material, and at worst a flagrant sampling of decontextualized forms, but it is definitely a significant mediator in contemporary practice. The past offers a toy chest of scrap from which designers can select the equivalent of costumes for dress up. Some religiously adhere to the historical models, and the verisimilitude of various Victorian, Art Nouveau, Art Deco, and Constructivist design makes it almost impossible to distinguish between the real and phony. Others use the past as a springboard to new discoveries. In the 1960s Push Pin Studios reprised Art Moderne (a.k.a. Art Deco) as "The Roxy Style," a hybrid of 1920s/30s decoration and sixties colors. In the 1980s Paula Scher recalled 1920s Russian Constructivism as an eclectic way of reintroducing viable design approaches considered passé or forgotten. And other designers simply return to the past (as presented in design annuals and magazines) for inspiration, borrowing or sampling bits and pieces for contemporary design. Much of the typographic nostalgia today focuses on the artifacts of commercial culture that have been made musty by time, but are charming by virtue of their age. Like playing with old toys encrusted with comparative innocence, toying with old types designed for comparatively more naive purposes will always have appeal.

NOSTALGIA

Book Jacket
The Lost Book of Paradise

Art Director
Victor Weaver

Designer
Carin Goldberg

Illustrator
Barbara Nessim

© *Hyperion Books* 1993

Book Cover
Ulysses

Art Director
Judith Loeser

Designer
Carin Goldberg

© *Vintage Books* 1986

Album Cover
Dvořák: Smetana

Art Director
Bob Hurwitz

Designer
Carin Goldberg

© *Nonesuch Records* 1986

Beer Label
Gorky's

Designers
Henry Vizcarra
Estay Heustis

© *Gorky's Russian Brewery* 1991

Book Jacket
The Divine Sarah

Designer
Louise Fili

© *Alfred A. Knopf* 1992

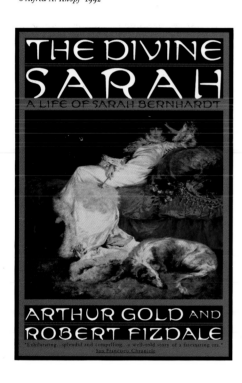

113

CD Package
The Very Very Best of
Dorsey Burnette

Art Director/Designer
Randall Martin

Illustrator
Peter Castro

© *Chrysalis Music
Group Inc.* 1991

Book Cover
The Gaga Years

Designer
Helene Silverman

© *Carol Publishing Group* 1992

114

Logo
Mudhoney

Designer
Art Chantry

© *Art Chantry* 1991

Magazine Spread
Rolling Stone

Art Director
Fred Woodward

Designer
Debra Bishop

Letterer
Anita Karl

Photographer
Kurt Marcus

© *Wenner Media, Inc.* 1990

Subway Poster
The S.S. Dragnet

Designers
Drew Hodges
Peter Mackey

© *Nickelodeon* 1991

Book Cover
Italian Art Deco

Art Director/Designer
Louise Fili

Typeface Designer
Jonathan Hoefler

© *Louise Fili* 1993

Poster
Modernism & Eclecticism

Art Director/Designer
Louise Fili

© *Louise Fili* 1992

115

Book Jacket
The Actual Adventures of
Michael Missing

Designer
Chip Kidd

Illustrator
Charles Burns

© *Chip Kidd* 1989

Book Cover
Pricing & Ethical Guidelines
Designer
Daniel Pelavin
© *Daniel Pelavin* 1991

Magazine Cover
Crossover Dreams
Designer
Daniel Pelavin
© *Daniel Pelavin* 1989

Album Cover
Showtime!
Designer
Carin Goldberg
© *EMI Records* 1982

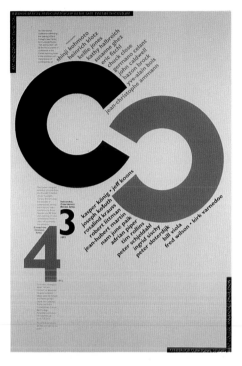

Poster
Bard

Art Director
Paula Scher

Designer
Ron Louie

© *Pentagram* 1992

Book Jacket
Family Values

Art Director
Frank Metz

Designer
Carin Goldberg

Illustrator
Ruth Steed

© *Simon & Schuster* 1993

Magazine Cover
Metropolis

Designers
Helene Silverman
Jeff Christensen

© *Metropolis* 1988

Book Jacket
King of the Wa-Kikuyu

Art Director
Henry Sene Yee

Designer
Angela Skouras

© *St. Martin's Press* 1993

CD Package
Crossfire

Art Directors
Ria Lewerke
Jackie Murphy

Designer
Sean Smith

Photographer
Maryellen McGrath

© *BMG Music and Reunion Records* 1983

Book Jacket
English Country House Murders

Designer
Miriam Campiz

© *Mysterious Press* 1990

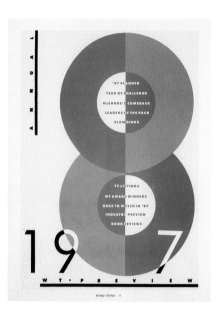

Magazine Page
World Tennis

Designer
Miriam Campiz

*© Media/World
Tennis* 1987

Newspaper Page
The Wall Street Journal

Art Director/Designer
Greg Leeds

Illustrator
Mick Wiggins

© Dow Jones & Co., Inc. 1990

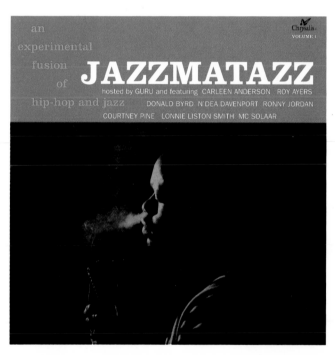

119

Album Cover
Jazzmatazz

Art Director
Henry Marquez

Designer
Diane Cuddy

Photographer
Humphry Studio

© EMI Records Group 1993

Book Jacket
Luncheon at the
Cafe Ridiculous

Art Director
Frank Metz

Designer
Carin Goldberg

Illustrator
Gene Greif

© Simon & Schuster 1988

Poster
Cult

Designer
Hugh Brown

© *ArtRock–San Francisco, CA* 1986

Book Jacket
Women on War

Art Director
Frank Metz

Designer
Carin Goldberg

Illustrator
Anthony Russo

© *Simon & Schuster* 1988

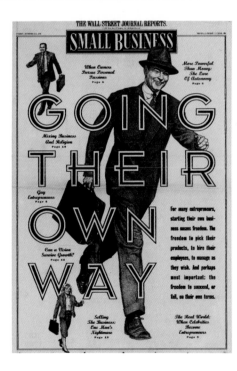

Newspaper Page
The Wall Street Journal

Art Director/Designer
Greg Leeds

Illustrator
Wendy Wray

© *Dow Jones & Co., Inc.* 1991

Poster
Dallas Texas

Art Director
Charles S. Anderson

Designers
Charles S. Anderson
Daniel Olson
Todd Hauswirth

*○ Charles S. Anderson
Design Company* 1991

Poster
C.S.A. Line Art Archive

Art Director
Charles S. Anderson

Designers
Charles S. Anderson
Todd Hauswirth
Daniel Olson

Illustrators
Charles S. Anderson
Randall Dahlk

*○ Charles S. Anderson
Design Company* 1992

Poster
AIGA T-Shirt Contest

Art Director
Charles S. Anderson

Designers
Charles S. Anderson
Todd Hauswirth

*○ Charles S. Anderson
Design Company* 1992

Invitation
Type 90

Designer
Jonathan Hoefler

© *The Hoefler Type Foundry, Inc.* 1990

☞ LECTURES

The core of Type90 will be a series of lectures and specialized 'town meetings,' short presentations followed by open discussions. There will be discussions of type history (including James Mosley's examination of antique ornamented types and John Dreyfus' chronicle of Charles Peignot), a look at the type of today (with presentations by post-post modernists Neville Brody and Zuzana Licko), and some predictions for the type of tomorrow (including Rene Kerfante and Günter Gerhard Lange on the future of type in Europe). Alan Jeeps of the BBC and Frans Lasès will discuss screen type in "The Good Morning Type Show," and Steven Heller will be leading an informal encounter group on "Truly Disgusting Novelty Faces and How to Use Them." Additional presentations will include typeface protection, type marketing for designers and foundries, and type education.

& TOWN MEETINGS

123

OXF☉RD

Home to the English-speaking world's oldest university, the "City of Dreaming Spires" is an intellectual paradise. With more than 900 buildings of historical and architectural importance within one square mile, Oxford's streets, houses, colleges and chapels (enhanced by gardens, croquet lawns and shaded tree-lined walks) showcase centuries of English history. There is no one building that dominates Oxford, no famous fortress or cathedral that offers a short-cut view of the city. The best way to get a feel for Oxford is to spend time wandering through the town, slowly taking it all in.

Type90 has arranged for rooms and meals at the colleges of Christ Church and Corpus Christi, located in central Oxford and near almost all Type90 events. For the best choice of housing, please fill out the reservation card as soon as possible, as hotel space will be extremely limited. PanAm has arranged competitive fares for Type90 attendees. To reach them in the U.S., call (800) 635-8470. Our conference code is CVN10005. Parking in Oxford is extremely limited; British Rail from London's Paddington Station and coach service from Heathrow Airport are quite suitable.

Type90 conferees are doers in real life, and a passive conference isn't what they want. Supplementing the lectures and town meetings will be a collection of workshops, offering an opportunity to be involved, to talk, and to explore in a more relaxed, social setting. Workshops will include "Type Design: The Master Class", Matthew Carter's celebrated workshop from Type 1987, featuring presentations by Sumner Stone, Günter Gerhard Lange and Gerard Unger. Paula Scher and Louise Fili will lead workshops on developing a personal design style with type, and Ronn Campisi and Aurobind Patel will open a discussion of type in publication design. Jim Parkinson will lead a workshop on logotype design, and Jonathan Hoefler will work with participants using type design tools for the Macintosh. John Benson, Lida Lopes Cardozo and David Kindersley will lead stone-cutting workshops, and John Downer will head a workshop on gold leaf signpainting. ¶ For the type-minded explorer, Type90 will include two playrooms stocked with every new tool for type design, typography and desktop publishing you care to get your hands on.

The *Association Typographique Internationale* Presents

TYPE 90

WE ARE AT AN IMPORTANT JUNCTURE in the history of type. Traditionally the domain of publishers, type is rapidly becoming a tool for everyone. ❧ A world conference, Type90, has been called this summer in Oxford to look at the issues from every possible angle, from aesthetic to technical to legal to lighthearted. ❧ For four days starting August 31, a whirlwind program of workshops, lectures, seminars and typographic events will be attended by an international panel of typophiles, from eminent type designers Matthew Carter and Adrian Frutiger, to leading graphic designers Neville Brody and Paula Scher, to type historians John Dreyfus and James Mosley, to typographic innovators Peter Karow and Rene Kerfante. ❧ In all, almost one hundred major typographers and designers have been invited to present their work, demonstrate techniques, and steer discussion. Type90 promises to be a truly unforgettable event. ❧

CD Package
Shut Up!

Designer
Art Chantry

Photographer
A. Patrick Adams

© *Art Chantry* 1993

124

Album Cover
Everyday Is a Holiday!

Designer
Art Chantry

© *Art Chantry* 1990

Album Cover
Ritual Dimension of
Sound

Designer
Art Chantry

Photographer
Scott Lindgren, "Coop"

© *Art Chantry/Estrus
Recording Institute* 1992

Album Cover
Clean as a Broke Dick Dog

Designer
Art Chantry

Photographer
Charles Peterson

© *Art Chantry/Sub Pop Records* 1992

Logo
The Big Life

Designer
STUDIO SEIREENI
Romane Cameron

Illustrator
Tim Clark

© Daiei Corporation 1992

THE DICK VAN DYKE SHOW

There are those who have called The Dick Van Dyke Show the best sitcom ever made. And it's hard to argue with them. Carl Reiner put together a program that defied all the rules of its era. He made Rob Petrie a real person with a real job that was integral to the story lines. He gave Rob and Laura a real marriage between equals, giving this ultimate classic the texture of real life. And then he put together one of the most solid ensembles ever. Mary Tyler Moore in her first comic role, Rose Marie, Morey Amsterdam, Jerry Paris, and, of course, our own Chairman, Dick Van Dyke.

The Mary Tyler Moore Show

And then there are those who say that this is the best sitcom ever. Again, it's hard to argue. The Mary Tyler Moore Show learned its lessons well from its classic predecessor and became a classic itself. Mary, Lou, Murray, Ted, Rhoda, Phyllis - those aren't characters. They're our friends. They're real people. And the things that happen to Mary - with parents, jobs, neighbors, lovers - are things we all go through. That's why we're happy to revisit Minneapolis and the WJM news room again and again. The Mary Tyler Moore Show is the classiest of classics.

DRAGNET

Is it a riveting crime drama? Is it minimalist art? Is it the most straight-shooting kitsch ever made? However you describe it, one thing is indisputably clear. Dragnet is a classic that has kept audiences glued to their sets for decades. Maybe it's the hypnotic Dum-de-dum-dum in the theme. Maybe it's Jack Webb's unshakeable resolve and implacable features. Or the fact that his character's name Friday reminds viewers of the weekend. No matter, Dragnet is an arresting member of the Nick at Nite lineup, and that's just the facts.

Media Kit
Nick at Nite

Designers
Michelle Willems
Mark Malabrigo

© Nick at Nite 1992

A pun is the humorous use of a word, or of words which are formed or sounded alike but have different meanings, in such a way as to play on two or more of the possible applications *(Webster's New World Dictionary of American Language)*. Likewise a typographic pun is a word or words that are

designed to underscore or enhance the meaning, by revealing two or more possible applications. This kind of visual pun is often created through the metamorphosis of a letterform into an image or object, but often the letterform simply substitutes for another word. Bradbury Thompson was a master at assigning letters with meaning. In one of his classic compositions from the 1940s he shows a baseball player hitting a home run. By using multiple settings of the letter O (the shape of a baseball) flying out off into space Thompson punned on the sound *OOOOOOOOOOOOUT*, as he vividly shows the ball flying OUT of the ballpark. Visual puns and typographic puns are among the most frequently used play-things in the designer's repertoire. In the quest to grab attention and convey a message puns are also the most economical way to convey complexity. But the successful pun is not less difficult in the visual than in verbal language. For Mesa, a Southwestern-style restaurant in New York, the logo uses a simple Gothic typeface with each capital letter in a different color. Though

eye-catching, what really made the logo memorable was the visual pun that was created by evenly cutting the tops of the letters off, thus making the word Mesa into a mesa. As with verbal language visual puns can engage the reader/viewer in a game of discovery.

¶uns

Logo
Bewear

Designer/Illustrator
BLACKDOG Mark Fox

© *Mark Fox/BlackDog* 1993

Logo
James Taylor
Deluxe Interstate '92

Art Director/Designer
Stephanie Mauer

© *Tisbury Tours* 1992

128

Logo
AIDS

Designers
Douglas G. Harp
Susan C. Harp

© *Douglas and Susan Harp* 1989

Magazine Spread Logo
Rolling Stone

Art Director
Fred Woodward

Designer
Gail Anderson

Letterer
Dennis Ortiz-Lopez

© *Wenner Media, Inc.* 1989

Logo
Fred

Designer
Fred Woodward

Letterer
Bill Gregg

© *Fred Woodward* 1980

Movie Logo
Ghost

Designer
FRANKFURT GIPS BALKIND
Peter Nguyen

© *Peter Nguyen* 1988

Poster
AZ You Like It

Art Directors
Forrest Richardson
Valerie Richardson

Designer
Forrest Richardson

Letterers
Forrest Richardson
Neill Fox

© *Richardson or Richardson* 1988

Book Cover
The New York Subway Finder

Designer/Letterer
Jon Valk

© *Stanhope Press* 1988

Logo
Manhattan Design

Designers
MANHATTAN DESIGN
Pat Gorman, Frank Olinsky

© *Pat Gorman & Frank Olinsky/*
Manhattan Design 1979

Book Cover
The Bridge Player's
Comprehensive
Guide to Defense

Art Director
Jackie Seow

Designer
Jon Valk

© *Fireside Books* 1990

130

Poster
Ambassador Arts: Letter P

Art Director
Paula Scher

Designers
Paula Scher
Ron Louie

© *Pentagram* 1993

Magazine Page
Agfa Magazine

Art Director
Paula Scher

Designer
Paula Scher

© *Pentagram* 1990

Poster
Oz ne

Art Director/Photographer
Douglas G. Harp

Designers
Douglas G. Harp
Susan C. Harp
Linda E. Wagner

© *Douglas G. Harp* 1993

131

Promotional Gift
Nick at Nite

Designer
Michelle Willems

© *Nick at Nite* 1993

Book Cover
The Mafia
Art Director/Designer/Illustrator
Peter Comitini
Unpublished 1992

Book Jacket
Inside the KGB
Designer
Henry Sene Yee
Illustrator
Ralph Wernli
© *Random House, Inc.* 1991

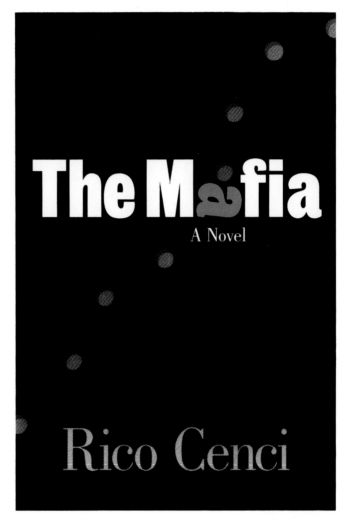

132

What ever happened to Mary Jo Kopechne's five girlfriends who had the good fortune *not* to drive off with Ted Kennedy? See page 37. Why has there never been a best-seller or a movie or even a television docudrama about Chappaquiddick? See page 40. In the age of Everythingscam and Whatevergate, how, after 18 years, can the Chappaquiddick cover-up remain so airtight? Good question. And why won't anybody publish an impressive new investigative book that for once gets a Kennedy cousin and Chappaquiddick witness *on the record* about the incident? Read this article.

EARLY IN THE MORNING of July 19, 1969, after attending an intimate party of male political cronies and female political aides, Senator Edward Kennedy drove his Oldsmobile off Chappaquiddick Island's Dyke Bridge and into Poucha Pond. His passenger, Mary Jo Kopechne, drowned.

This is not exactly news. Most of us recall that after a considerable public tumpus, Senator Kennedy took the extraordinary step of going on television to explain—altogether unconvincingly—this latest Kennedy tragedy.

Kennedy pleaded guilty to leaving the scene of an accident after causing personal injury and later promised to

CHAPPAQUIDDICK

The Unsold Story

BY TAD FRIEND

consider resigning his Senate seat (*Nahh&é*, he evidently decided, instead going on to win reelection three times).

After receiving a two-month suspended sentence, he clammed up. And so did everyone else in a position to fill in some of the blanks—the five women at the party who did not drown in Ted Kennedy's car, the five men at the party who did not swim away from a submerged Oldsmobile and then lie about it. So the inquiries have blundered along without Kennedy's help, or the help of his loyal friends at the party. And so, naturally, strange Chappaquiddick theories abound: Kennedy was driving; Kennedy wasn't driving; Kennedy murdered Kopechne because she was pregnant with his child, and jumped out of the moving car in the nick of time; and so on.

What is news—or should be—is that Joe Gargan, a cousin of Kennedy's who spent much of that fatal evening with the senator, finally did unburden himself of his Chappaquid-

Magazine Spread
Spy
Art Director/Designer
Alexander Isley
© *Spy* 1987

"This is as far as I go," choked the pilot. "Any closer, we're gonna be marshmallows at a campfire."

Maybe he was right, but I simply had to have the shot.

"Another fifty feet," I replied, the hot sulfur fumes burning my eyes as I squinted through the camera.

"Get me down fifty feet and we'll have it."

Suddenly, the boiling magma below us exploded, twisting us sideways and downward.

Ten yards away a fountain of lava burst into the sky, narrowly missing us as I scrambled to re-focus.

We seemed to be out of control, spinning into the fiery maw of certain death.

Next to me, the pilot frantically pushed through a dozen Hail Marys.

"I whispered to

Poster
Science Museum of
Minnesota

Designer
Sue Crolick

© *Sue Crolick Advertising and
Design* 1991

Stationery
Joan Ostrin

Designer
Sue Crolick

© *Sue Crolick Advertising and
Design* 1990

133

Stationery
Sue Crolick

Designer
Sue Crolick

© *Sue Crolick Advertising and
Design* 1982

Invitation
HELL-O & Happy Holidays

Designer
Vincent Sainato

© *Spot Design* 1992

T-Shirts
Formal-i-T
Casual-T

Designer
Jack Summerford

© *Summerford Design, Inc.* 1993

134

Magazine Cover
Newsweek

Art Director/Designer
Peter Comitini

© *Newsweek, Inc. All right reserved.*
Reprinted by permission 1990.

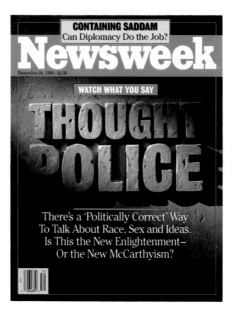

Summerford Design, Inc.
Summerford Design, Inc.
Summerford Design, Inc.
Summerford Design, Inc.
Summerford Design, Inc.
2706 Fairmount
Dallas 75201
214 748 4638
Jack

Logo
Summerford Design, Inc.

Designer
Jack Summerford

© *Jack Summerford* 1991

**Record & CD
Packages**
Forestry

Art Directors
David Byrne
Robin Lynch

Designer
Robin Lynch

© *Sire Records* 1991

135

Stationery
Little City

Designer
Bruce Yelaska

© *Bruce Yelaska* 1987

MESA
GRILL

Magazine Spread
Spy

Art Director
Alexander Isley

Designer
Catherine Gilmore-Barnes

© *Spy* 1988

Logo
Mesa Grill

Art Director
Alexander Isley

Designer
Alexander Knowlton

© *Mesa Grill* 1990

Promotional Template
Isley Architects
Place and Trace

Designer
Alexander Isley

© *Isley Architects Inc.* 1986

Logo
American Museum of
the Moving Image

Designer
Alexander Isley

Illustrator
Kam Mak

© *Alexander Isley* 1991

Journal
BAM New Music America

Art Director
Alexander Isley

Designer
Alexander Knowlton

© *Brooklyn Academy of Music* 1988

In the 1980s the term vernacular, referring to a common language, was adopted by graphic designers who, in rejecting the slick professionalism of commercial Modernism borrowed, reappropriated, and celebrated the "dirty design" typical of the anonymous commercial artist. In a culture that is dominated by commerce, certain standards—easy, non-threatening design clichés—have developed over time to help identify and sell products. Such approaches were dubbed non-design by Modern professionals. But with the advent of the Post-Modern professional such artlessness has become a virtue, and the basis for new purposefully naïf design. In this context one could call indigenous the work of the typical sign painter. Craftspeople have been heroicized as "street artists." However, in addition to commercial street art, there is also a subcultural street art that is at odds with it. Graffiti is the principal street expression. It is illegally rendered, usually in public view on private surfaces. Graffiti has always been a personal mark. "Killroy Was Here," perhaps the world's most famous graffito, was a way for an otherwise anonymous individual to make a mark. Today graffiti is also a cultural manifestation of the disenfranchised, people who want to speak out (if only to speak at all) but do not have the official means of address. Graffiti is the ultimate vernacular, yet it is expressed in various styles and mannerisms. For despite the deliberate anonymity of its creators, graffiti is very much about publicizing oneself. It is curious, but not altogether surprising that graffiti in its variegated forms became yet another plaything for the professional designer. Scavenging from the street became a form of play, and then what was scavenged was combined with more formal design elements. Eventually vernacular became a marketable style, rather than a reflection of real cultural diversity.

138

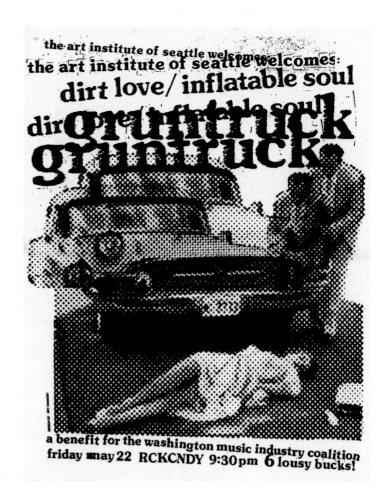

the art institute of seattle welcomes
the art institute of seattle welcomes:

dir gruntruck
gruntruck

a benefit for the washington music industry coalition
friday may 22 RCKCNDY 9:30pm 6 lousy bucks!

Poster
Mudhoney

Designer
Art Chantry

© *Art Chantry* 1991

Poster
Gruntruck

Designer
Art Chantry

© *Art Chantry* 1991

140

the art institute of seattle welcomes

mudhoney
flop / the gits!
a chicken soup brigade benefit

rckcndy friday feb. twenty-eighth

YOUR COMMENTS HERE:

Ticketmaster

CD
Eat Your Heart Out

Art Directors
Jane Gulick
David Scharff

Designer
TWELVE POINT RULE

Record Company
Matador Records

© *TVT Music* 1993

Poster
Coca 1991 Season

Designer
Art Chantry

© *Art Chantry* 1991

CD Package
You're Always Welcome

Designer
Art Chantry

© *Art Chantry/Lucky Records* 1993

LIVE IN THE BUCKLE OF THE BIBLE BELT
FREE ADMISSION   FREE ADMISSION

CREATIVE REVIVAL CRUSADE

PORTFOLIO CENTER

ASSEMBLY HALL
125 BENNETT ST., ATLANTA, GEORGIA

THURS., SEPT. 23, 1993

YOUR DEVOTED FOLLOWERS
AWAIT THE TRAIN
TO THE PROMISED LAND

2:00 P.M. - READ THE GOOD BOOKS
4:00 - 6:00 P.M. - MEET THEIR MAKERS
8:00 P.M. - FINAL BLESSING OF GRADUATES
COME EXPECTING A MIRACLE AND LEAVE WITH A CHOSEN FEW
SEE THE LIGHT!   SEE THE BOOKS!

TO WITNESS, CALL
CAROL VICK AT 1-800-255-3169

Creative Two Drink Minimum C.W. Susan Treacy, A.D. Todd Gallentine/ Typesetting and Printing Southern Poster

Poster
Creative Revival

Creative Director
Roger Richards

Art Director
Todd Gallentine

Typesetting
Southern Poster

© *Portfolio Center* 1992

CD/Package
Ain't No Other

Art Director
Lynn Kowalewski

Photographer
Merlyn Rosenberg

© *Atlantic Recording Corp./*
First Priority Music 1993

Tabloid Cover
Northwest Extra!

Designer
Art Chantry

Illustrator
Robert Crumb

© *Art Chantry* 1989

143

Poster
New City Theater

Designer
Art Chantry

© *Art Chantry* 1990

Poster
Czechoslovakian Printmakers

Designer
Art Chantry

© *Art Chantry* 1989

Logos
Bark Promo Cards
Designers
SMOKEBOMB STUDIO
Nancy Mazzei, Brian Kelly

© *Smokebomb Studio* 1992

Poster
Cramps
Designer/Illustrator
Philip Cooper

© *ArtRock–San Francisco, CA* 1989

CD Package
Taurus No Bull
Designers
SMOKEBOMB STUDIO
Nancy Mazzei, Brian Kelly

© *TVT Records* 1993

Poster
AmRep 1992 CMJ Showcase
Designer
Frank Kozik

© *Frank Kozik c/o ArtRock–
San Francisco, CA* 1992

RHYMES/ANN SALWEY
DRAWINGS/FRAN BULL

RHYMES FOR MODERN TIMES

JACK BE NIMBLE

JACK BE QUICK

SHRED ALL THE EVIDENCE

Quick, Quick, Quick!

AS I WAS COMING DOWN THE STAIR

I MET A MAN WHO WASN'T THERE.

HE WAVED A PAPER CUP AT ME $$

WHICH I WAS ABLE NOT TO SEE.

HE WASN'T THERE AGAIN TODAY

I WISH THAT MAN WOULD GO AWAY!

146

Book Spreads
Mordant Rhymes for Modern Times

Designer
Yolanda Cuomo

Illustrator
Fran Bull

Woodtype Handsetter
Gwynne Truglio

© *Fran Bull* 1990

THIS IS THE HOUSE THAT

CRACK BUILT

This is the drug
That lay in the house that Crack built.
This is the rat who sold the drug
That lay in the house that Crack built.
This is the cat who needed the shot
And bought from the rat
Who sold the drug
That lay in the house that Crack built.
This is the cop who worried the cat
Who needed the shot
And bought from the rat
Who sold the drug
That lay in the house that Crack built.
This is the man all tattered and torn
Who shot the cop who worried the cat
Who needed the shot
And bought from the rat who sold the drug
That lay in the house that Crack built.
This is the maiden all forlorn
Who carries a baby yet unborn
By the tattered man who killed the cop
Who worried the cat
Who needed the shot
And bought from the rat who sold the drug
That lay in the house that Crack built.

Logo
Tad

Designer
Art Chantry

© Art Chantry 1991

FULGHUM HEAVY IND*USTRIES*

Letterhead Imprint
Fulghum Heavy Industries

Designer
Art Chantry

© Art Chantry 1990

Logo
Artists' Products

Designer
Art Chantry

© Art Chantry 1989

the outline of a head, or an R, B, or H are the body), or as a pure pun (i.e. the letters that make up the face or body can also be read as a word or phrase). Typeface design can be as easy as children's art, or as complex as a Cubist collage. Regardless, the aim is to have fun with, indeed tweak the senses of the viewer. Type faces are not appropriate for all design problems, but given their frequency in design annuals and shows, the face is certainly one of the most popular typographic toys on the market.

T

he face is the most expressive of our dramatic and comedic tools, and making silly faces is a fundamental part of the play instinct. Likewise making faces from letterforms is key to contemporary typeplay. A type face is the ultimate pun since all the letters serve other functions. However, within the typeface *discipline* numerous approaches are practiced. Among them, type used simply as line or shape (i.e. Os for eyes, T for nose, G for ears, and Xs for hair), or metamorphosed into a face (i.e. a G, Q, or O is used as

Book Jacket
Uncommon Wisdom

Art Director/Designer
Paula Scher

© *Pentagram* 1988

Magazine Page
Rolling Stone

Art Director
Fred Woodward

Designer
Debra Bishop

Letterer
Anita Karl

© *Wenner Media, Inc.* 1991

Brochure
Type That Talks

Designers
Jeff Fabian
Sam Shelton
Jean Kane

© *KINETIK* 1989

Magazine Page
Rolling Stone

Art Director/Designer
Fred Woodward

Letterer
Anita Karl

© *Wenner Media, Inc.* 1992

Poster
Moving Announcement

Art Directors
Takaaki Matsumoto
Michael McGinn

Designer
Takaaki Matsumoto

© *M Plus M, Incorporated* 1989

Advertisement
Gilbert Paper

Designer
THIRST Rick Valicenti

© *THIRST* 1992

151

152

The Executive Committee of the New York Chapter of The American Institute of Graphic Arts cordially invites you to attend the members' opening of the

Co**mm**u**n**ic**atio**n **G**rap**hi**c**s**

(Refreshments will be served)

s**ho**w

Wednesday, May 17, 1989 5:30–7:30 pm, The AIGA Gallery, 1059 3rd Avenue at 63rd St., New York. This invitation admits a New York Chapter member to the opening. IT MUST BE PRESENTED AT THE DOOR. Admission is $8 for guests and members who do not bring invitations. The exhibition will be open to the public Monday through Friday, 9:30 am to 4:45 pm, through June 16th. *AIGA***NY**

Annual Report Logo
Dallas Zoological Society

Designer
Scott Ray

© *Peterson & Company* 1990

THE JOYS OF TOYS

TOYS

AT THE GALLERIA

theGalleria Presents The Eveready Holiday Toytown
Over 300 Battery-Operated Toys · Hands On Display
Thursday · Sunday · November 12 · November 15
Galleria I · Ice Rink Level · FREE TO THE PUBLIC

Poster
Toys

Creative Director
THE HILL GROUP Chris Hill

Designer
David Lerch

© *The Hill Group* 1987

153

Poster
Zoot Restaurant

Designer
Lana Rigsby

© *Rigsby Design* 1991

Poster
Öola

Art Director
Paula Scher

Designers
Paula Scher
Debra Bishop

© *Pentagram* 1990

154

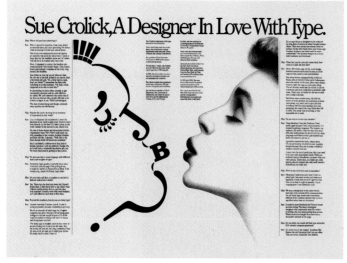

Magazine Spread
May Typography Quarterly

Designer
Sue Crolick

© *Sue Crolick Advertising and Design* 1990

Logo
Culinary Productions, Inc.

Designer
BENNETT PEJI DESIGN
Bennett Peji

© *Bennett Peji* 1990

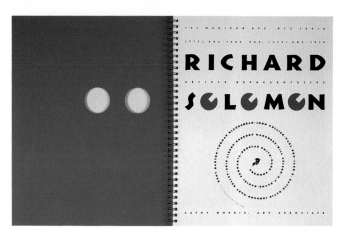

Magazine Cover
The Boston Globe Magazine

Designers
Terry Allen
Lucy Bartholomay

Illustrator
Terry Allen

Typography
Lucy Bartholomay

© *The Boston Globe Newspaper Co.* 1991

Promotional Book Cover/Spread
Richard Solomon

Art Director/Designer
Louise Fili

© *Richard Solomon* 1992

Logo
JCH TeleGraphics

Art Directors
Takaaki Matsumoto
Michael McGinn

Designer
Michael McGinn

© *M Plus M, Incorporated* 1988

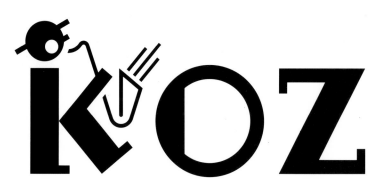

Logo
Embarko

Designer/Illustrator/Letterer
BLACKDOG Mark Fox

© *Mark Fox/BlackDog* 1989

Logo
Dave Koz

Art Directors
Tommy Steele
Jeff Fey

Designer/Illustrator
BLACKDOG Mark Fox

© *Mark Fox/BlackDog* 1990

156

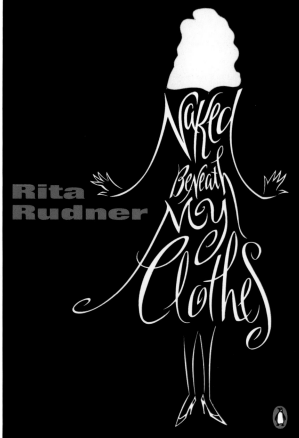

Book Cover
Naked Beneath My Clothes

Art Director
Michael Ian Kaye

Designer
Robert Clyde Anderson

Photographer
Kenneth Bank

© *Viking Penguin* 1993

Book Cover
Inside the KGB
Designer/Illustrator
Peter Comitini
Unpublished 1992

Book Cover
Annie Lennox
Art Director
Henry Sene Yee
Designer
Angela Skouras
Photographer
RETNA Lewis Ziolek
© *St. Martin's Press* 1993

On-Air Logos
MTV Ears
MTV Eyeball
Designer
Pat Gorman
© *Pat Gorman (MTV)* 1989

Contrary to the Bible, in the beginning was the image. If one is to accept theories of prehistory over those of religious doctrine, the spoken word took time to evolve and the written word did not catch on right away, either. The Lascaux caves contain the evidence of the primitive's need to express through marks that comment on the environment. One can imagine the caveperson's frustration at not being able to further amplify these visual ideas with verbal language. Despite the expressive power of the grunt, being able to combine words into sentences and paragraphs to illustrate the picture might have pushed back the discovery of charades by millennia, but would have considerably increased the ability to effortlessly communicate. It is not surprising that after the word came and writing developed there was a primal need to embellish it with images, for words alone were not enough to communicate The Word. Manuscript illuminators of old commanded inflated hourly rates for it was commonly believed that readers needed the inducement of an image to enter into reading a text. And yet even back then there was a tension between editor and art director over the ratio of text versus image. The illuminated initial was developed as a means of combining letter and picture into a single image. The invention of type in the sixteenth century was a boon to mass communications but the death knell of complex illumination. The technology simply did not allow for the total integration of letter and picture. During the sixteenth century, advances in typography further eroded this relationship.

The separation of illustration and ornament from type was common until the nineteenth century, when artists of the Art Nouveau movement and the poster revolution of the Belle Epoch wed hand-drawn letters with art. Shortly after, the Aesthetic and Arts and Crafts movements reprised certain Medieval styles of integrated type and image. And yet despite these historical roots the total integration of type and image is a Modern invention. Advanced printing technology and reverence for machine-made art made it possible to join the two elements into one composition. The marriage of type and image is the cornerstone of graphic design, and nothing can tear it asunder.

TYPE &

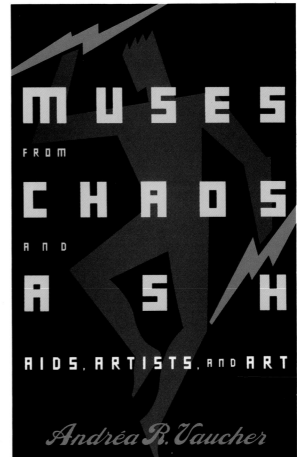

Book Jacket
Muses from Chaos and Ash
Art Director
Krystyna Skalski
Designer
Carin Goldberg
© *Grove Press* 1992

Greeting Card
New Year Greeting
Designer
Rebeca Mendez
© *Art Center College of Design* 1989

Magazine Cover
Time
Art Director/Designer
Mirko Ilic
© *Time Warner Inc.* 1991

Poster
Bathhouse Theatre
Designer
Art Chantry
© *Art Chantry* 1983

Magazine Cover
Emigre
Art Director/Designer
Rudy Vanderlans
© *Emigre* 1992

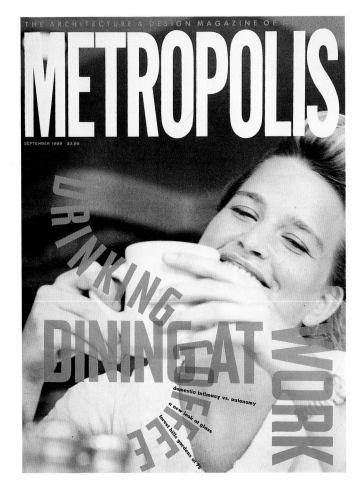

THE ARCHITECTURE & DESIGN MAGAZINE OF

METROPOLIS

SEPTEMBER 1988 $3.95

DRINKING
DINING EAT WORK
SLEE

domestic intimacy vs. autonomy

a new look at glass

forest hills gardens at 75

Magazine Cover
Metropolis

Art Director/Designer
Helene Silverman

Photographer
Kristine Larsen

© *Metropolis* 1988

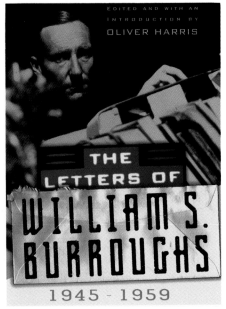

Logos
Byron Priess Multimedia

Art Director
Paula Scher

Designers
Paula Scher
Ron Louie

162   © *Pentagram* 1993

Book Jacket
The Letters of
William S. Burroughs

Designer
Paul Buckley

Photographer
Allen Ginsbergh

© *Penguin USA* 1993

Record Sleeve
Fast Piss Blues/I Got the Blues

Art Director/Letterer
Robert Hamilton

Illustrator
Roderigo Avila

© *Matador Records* 1992

Poster
Greenleaf Medical

Art Director/Designer/Letterer
Earl Gee

Photographer
Geoffrey Nelson

© *Earl Gee Design* 1990

Poster
December Calendar

Art Director
Lisa Levin

Designer
Ashlie Benton

© *Lisa Levin* 1992

Book Jacket
Olga: Revolutionary and Martyr

Art Director
Krystyna Skalski

Designer
Carin Goldberg

© *Grove Press* 1989

Magazine Page
Rolling Stone

Art Director
Fred Woodward

Designer
Debra Bishop

Photographer
Doug Rosa

© *Wenner Media, Inc.* 1993

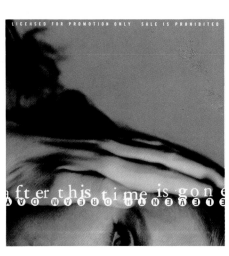

Promotional CD/Package
After This Time Is Gone

Art Director
Melanie Nissen

Designer
Frank Gargiulo

Photographer
Amy Guip

© *Atlantic Recording Corp.* 1993

Book Jacket
A Good Scent from a
Strange Mountain

Art Directors
Krystyna Skalski
Raquel Jaramillo

Designer
Carin Goldberg

Illustrator
Neil Flewellen

© *Henry Holt* 1992

Book Jacket
A Visit Home

Art Director
Frank Metz

Designer
Carin Goldberg

Photographer
Barry Marcus

© *Simon & Schuster* 1993

Book Jacket
The Great German Films

Designer
Louise Fili

© *Louise Fili* 1991

Book Jacket
The Place in Flowers
Where Pollen Rests

Art Director
Alex Gotfryd

Designer
Carin Goldberg

© *Doubleday* 1988

Book Jacket
This Day and Age

Designer
Archie Ferguson

Photographer
Diana Klein

© *Alfred A. Knopf* 1992

166

Book Jacket
Hole in the Sky

Art Director
Carol Devine Carson

Designer
Barbara de Wilde

Photographer
Kurt Marcus

© *Alfred A. Knopf* 1992

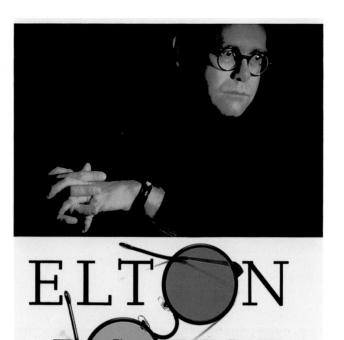

Book Jacket
Elton John: The Biography

Art Director
John Fontana

Designer
Henry Sene Yee

Photographers
LONDON FEATURES INT'L.
P. Ollern Shaw
Katherine Mc Gylnn *still life*

© *Harmony Books, a division of*
Crown Publishers, Inc. 1992

Book Jacket
Motor City

Designer
Archie Ferguson

© *Alfred A. Knopf* 1992

167

Book Jacket
A Poet's Bible

Art Director
Victor Weaver

Designer
Carin Goldberg

Illustrator
Melanie Marder Parks

© *Hyperion Books* 1992

Invitation Booklet
Tuna and Pat's Wedding

Art Director
Pat Gorman

Illustrator
Lynda Barry

© *Pat Gorman* 1989

Book Cover
Head Comix

Art Director
Stacey Holston

Designer/Illustrator
R. Crumb

© *R. Crumb* 1987

Album Cover
Big World

Designer
ROSENWORLD Laurie Rosenwald

Illustrator
Serge Clerc

© *A&M Records* 1986

Book Cover
Bring the Noise

Art Director
John Fontana

Designer/Letterer
Henry Sene Yee

© *Harmony Books, a division of Crown Publishers, Inc.* 1991

Album Cover
Free South Africa

Designer
Art Chantry

© *Art Chantry/Out Front Music* 1990

Brochure
CLaGS

Designer
Chip Kidd

© *Chip Kidd* 1988

Brochure
Stat Store Capabilities

Art Director/Designer
Alexander Isley

© *Stat Store* 1988

Book Jacket
Fish Boy

Designers
Chip Kidd
Barbara de Wilde

© *Chip Kidd and Barbara de Wilde* 1991

Ad Series
Greenleaf Medical

Art Director/Designer/Letterer
Earl Gee

Photographer
Geoffrey Nelson

© *Earl Gee Design* 1992

The invention of the typewriter in the late nineteenth century was as revolutionary as that of the personal computer in the late twentieth and posed many of the same challenges. In addition to conceiving and manufacturing a mechanism for this remarkable writing machine, the question of what letterforms it should include had to have been a major issue. The decision to use the two slab serif faces (pica and elite) defined the look of business communications for over a century. Although variations on the form were designed over time, the basic appearance of a typewritten page did not significantly change—even after IBM introduced its replaceable golf ball with numerous other typestyles—until the advent of the word processor. Typewriter type became forever associated with personal or business writing, while type foundry faces were, of course, the exclusive province of professional printing. The distinction was so ingrained that, although American Typefoundry offered *American Typewriter* as a hot metal cut in various sizes and weights, it was only used professionally when a typographer wanted to evoke informal formality. Commercial artists preferred the standard types to typewriter because the latter did not command authority on the printed page. And yet certain Modern designers from the 1930s found in actual typewriter type the same kind of naively expressive quality that early Macintosh typographers found in low resolution dot matrix type. Among the masters of the Modern, Alexey Brodovitch and Paul Rand produced seminal compositions that used typewriter type to express their rebellion against traditional typography. After they opened the gates, typewriter became a very common way for designers to express immediacy. Today with thousands of fonts available to the average secretary, more formal faces are being used instead of typewriter type. Probably in time this ubiquitously popular face will become as anachronistic as Old English or Fraktur, but it will always be the most democratic of the world's faces.

TXXYPE - WRITER TYPE

what's in a face
and
what's beneath those eyes
is this for real
or
is it merely a disguise

deeper
than
skin

is the
beauty
eye admire

deeper than skin

is the love i desire

Invitation
DIFFA
Designers
Jeff Fabian
Laura Latham
Sam Shelton
Photographer
Geof Kern
© *DIFFA DC* 1991

something wonderful happens silent auction throughout the evening 6:30 pm dinner guests arrive 9 pm party guests arrive 10 pm fashion show 11pm dancing

174

Logo
VH-1 Classic Rock
Designer
SMOKEBOMB STUDIO Nancy Mazzei
© *VH-1* 1991

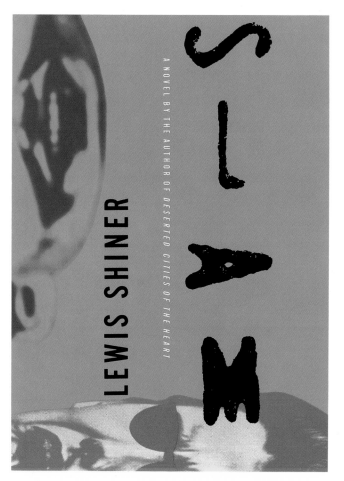

Book Jacket
Slam

Designer
Chip Kidd

© *Chip Kidd* 1990

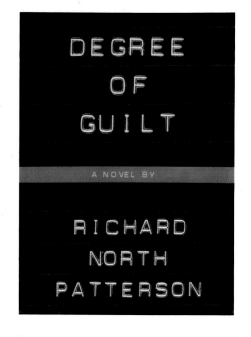

Book Jacket
Degree of Guilt

Art Director/Designer
Carol Devine Carson

© *Alfred A. Knopf* 1993

175

Book Cover
Edge City

Designer
Paul Buckley

© *Penguin USA* 1993

Magazine Cover
Rolling Stone

Art Director/Designer
Fred Woodward

Photographer
Herb Ritts

© *Wenner Media, Inc.* 1992

Book Jacket
Breaking Blue

Designer
Barbara de Wilde

Photographer
Geoff Spear

© *Barbara de Wilde* 1991

Book Jacket
Life Sketches

Designer
Archie Ferguson

© *Alfred A. Knopf* 1989

Magazine Spread
Rolling Stone

Art Director
Fred Woodward

Designer
Angela Skouras

Illustrator
Everett Peck

© *Wenner Media, Inc.* 1992

Poster
Low Technology
Designer
Art Chantry

© *Art Chantry* 1989

Book Cover
No Mercy
Designer
Frank Gargiulo
Photographer
Jerald Frampton

© *Atlantic Monthly Press* 1989

Typeface Specimen
Back Spacer
Designer
SMOKEBOMB STUDIO
Nancy Mazzei, Brian Kelly

© *Smokebomb Studio* 1993

CD Package
The Silent Majority
Designers
P. Scott Makela
Debora Norcross
Photographer
Amy Guip

© *Warner Bros. Records* 1992

Book Cover
Great Jones Street
Designer
Michael Ian Kaye
Photographer
Ralph Gibson

© *Penguin* 1994

Chapter 17

Typography serves the word, and the word communicates ideas. After all the typeplay, after all the transcendent notions of graphic design as art, in the final analysis type is an instrument of meaning, and typography is its structural manifestation. However, in the end the arrangement is irrelevant—centered, flush left, flush right, symmetrical or asymmetrical, are choices that contribute to the aesthetics of a design. Rather what is important is how clearly the word, and ultimately the message, is presented. But even this is debatable. Classical humanist typography is devoted to making words accessible. Post-Modern deconstructivist typography is concerned with making words emote. What is more important, and to whom? Should everyone read the same words in the same way, or should room be set aside for ambiguity and nuance? This is the most significant question concerning typography today. In the final analysis style is no more or less than an accent. The world is comprised of countless languages, so why should typography be limited to a few accents? The Modern's mission to universalize language was not all that different from the Church's mission to convert the heathens—and rid them of their cultural difference. Cultures have their own beliefs, ethics, rituals, and languages. But even in most primitive or ancient languages there are equivalent words (or signs) in other languages. While the curse of Babel—the plethora of languages—might seem counterproductive in terms of global intercourse, in fact each language contributes to the worldview. Likewise typography need not be constricted by the neutrality imposed by some global idealism. What is key to effective typography is not that strict rules are obeyed, or for that matter, challenged, but that meaning is conveyed effectively. In this sense it is important to address the basics, the fundamental concern of language and its servants. Exploring how the word alone is communicated is the most basic issue in typography.

THE WORD

Remember our old parties?

People punched holes in the walls.

They put cigarettes out on the floor.

They peed in the sink.

But now, we own the place.

Invitation
Remember Our Old Parties?

Designer
Sue Crolick

© Sue Crolick Advertising and Design 1992

Film Title
Heaven and Las Vegas

Designers/Photographers
REVERB
Somi Kim, Lisa Nugent

© Somi Kim and Lisa Nugent 1990

RADIO

Make your designs irresistible with unusual or
out-of-the-ordinary character treatments.
Never pass up an opportunity to give the
reader more than they bargained for!

COOL

A steady hand and some imagination are the
only tools you need to achieve really striking
results. This design looks particularly
refreshing thanks to a judicious use of white
to create an "icy" effect.

OVER

BOWLERAMA

This technique combines a delicate use of
proportion with a careful attention to detail and
should only be attempted by the most
advanced commercial artists.

HEAT

Feel free to exaggerate to make a point. In this
case, shooting flames and "rippled"
typography make a much more memorable
impression than, say, a glowing ember
or a matchstick.

OVER

Shadow

A truly talented studio designer will always resist
the temptation to over-design. In this instance,
the ever-popular drop shadow is used not
as an accent, but to actually spell out the
entire word.

HORROR!

In this more advanced treatment, the usage of
"shaky" or "chattering" characters gives the
reader an uneasy feeling, creating exactly
the sought-after impression.

OVER

Advertising Insert
French Paper Company

Art Directors/Designers
Charles S. Anderson
Daniel Olson

Illustrator
Randall Dahlk

© *French Paper Company* 1989

THE MAGAZINE FOR MEN

FEBRUARY 1992·$2.50

WHITE PEOPLE

THE TROUBLE WITH AMERICA

Magazine Covers
Newsweek

Designer
Peter Comitini

182

Magazine Cover
Esquire

Art Director
Rhonda Rubinstein

Designer
Roger Black

Magazine Cover
Esquire

Designer
Barbara Kruger

Photographer
Dave Pokress

© *Esquire Magazine* 1992

The Boston Globe Magazine
OCTOBER 27, 1991

I thought you were picking up the kids. Wait'll you hear about *my* day. We need some time alone. I'll pencil you in. What do you mean, *my* cat? I'm too tired. I was in a meeting. *You* pick up the baby sitter. Not takeout again. I'm too tired. Guilt is my middle name. I thought we talked last month. **THE TRUTH ABOUT DUAL-CAREER FAMILIES** Just because you make more money doesn't make you God. I'm not a mind reader. I'm too tired. Fine, *you* do the shopping from now on. If I make an appointment, will you pay attention to me? What makes you think I'm going to move? *You* have the baby. I'm too tired. So you vacuumed – big deal. When did you turn into my mother? *You* stay home and wait for the plumber. **BY ALISON BASS** I don't have time to be sick. I'm too tired. Those *can't* be chicken pox. What did I do to deserve children like you? My father never cooked. How do you feel about taking separate vacations? I'm too tired. Let me get back to you.

Magazine Cover
The Boston Globe Magazine

Designer/Typography
Lucy Bartholomay

© *The Boston Globe Newspaper Co.* 1991

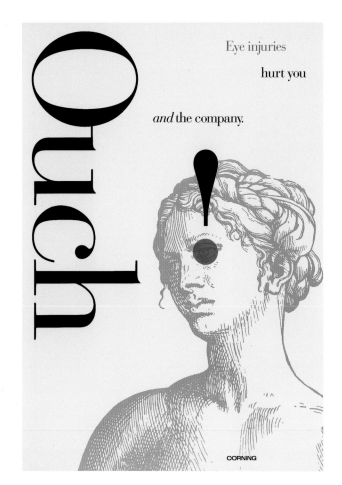

Eye injuries

hurt you

and the company.

CORNING

Safety Posters
Ouch!

Art Director
Douglas G. Harp

Designers
Douglas G. Harp
CORNING CORPORATE DESIGN

Illustrator
Andreas Vesalius

© *Corning Incorporated* 1988

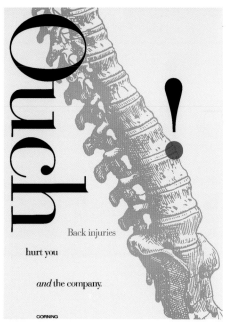

Back injuries

hurt you

and the company.

CORNING

Hand injuries

hurt you

and the company.

CORNING

184

Poster
THINK

Designer
Gail Anderson

Letterer
Dennis Ortiz-Lopez

© *Visual Perceptions* 1990

SIT

EAT

GO TO THE BATHROOM

Brochure
AIGA Awards Ceremony

Designer
Jack Summerford

© *American Institute of Graphic Arts* 1989

Appendix

ABCD
854 West 181 Street, #6D
New York, NY 10033
Anthony Bloch

Alfred A. Knopf Inc.
201 East 50th Street
New York, NY 10022
Carol Devine Carson
Barbara de Wilde
Archie Ferguson
Chip Kidd

Charles S. Anderson Design Company
30 North First Street
Minneapolis, MN 55401
Charles S. Anderson
Randall Dahlk
Todd Hauswirth
Daniel Olson

Art Center College of Design
1700 Lida Street
Pasadena, CA 91103
Rebeca Mendez

ArtRock
1153 Mission Street
San Francisco, CA 94103
Hugh Brown
Frank Kozik

Atlantic Records
1290 6th Avenue, 4th Floor
New York, NY 10019
Lee Bates
Charlie Becker
Jean Cronin
Frank Gargiulo

Atlantic Records
75 Rockefeller Plaza
New York, NY 10019
Lynn Kowalewski

Richard Baker
161 West 16th Street, #165
New York, NY 10011

Bar / None Records Inc.
One Newark Street
Hoboken, NJ 07030
Steve Boyd
Glenn Morrow
Lisa Wagner

BlackDog
239 Marin Street
San Rafael, CA 94901
Mark Fox

The Boston Globe
135 Morrissey Boulevard
Boston, MA 02193
Terry Allen
Lucy Bartholomay
Rena Sokolow

Studio Bustamante
2400 Keitner Boulevard, #226
San Diego, CA 92101
Gerald Bustamante

Leslie Cabarga
258 West Tulpehocken Street
Germantown, PA 19144

Miriam Campiz
165 West 66th Street
New York, NY 10023

David Carson Design
128¹/₂ 10th Street
Del Mar, CA 92014

Castle Systems
1306 Lincoln Avenue
San Rafael, CA 74901-2105
Jason Castle

Art Chantry Design
P.O. Box 4069
Seattle, WA 98104

Margo Chase Design
2255 Bancroft Avenue
Los Angeles, CA 90039

Chermayeff & Geismar, Inc.
15 East 26th Street, 12th Floor
New York, NY 10010
Cathy Schaefer

Peter Comitini Design
30 Waterside Plaza
New York, NY 10010

David Cowles
775 Landing Road North
Rochester, NY 14625

Sue Crolick Advertising & Design
Lumber Exchange Building, Suite 700
10 South Fifth Street
Minneapolis, MN 55402

Yolanda Cuomo Design
515 West 19th Street
New York, NY 10011

Cyclone Communications & Design
107 South Street
Boston, MA 02111
Robert Hamilton

Barry Deck Design
611 Broadway, #840
New York, NY 10012

Elektra Records
75 Rockefeller Plaza
New York, NY 10019
Robin Lynch

Emigre
4475 "D" Street
Sacramento, CA 95819
Anne Burdicke
Gail Swanlund
Rudy Vanderlans

ERG
1290 Avenue of the Americas
New York, NY 10104
Marc Cozza

Esquire
250 West 55th Street
New York, NY 10019
Roger Black
Amid Capeci
Barbara Kruger
Rhonda Rubinstein

Louise Fili Ltd.
22 West 19th Street
New York, NY 10011

Frankfurt Balkind Partners
244 East 58th Street
New York, NY 10022
Danny Abelson
Aubrey Balkind
Thomas Bricker
Andreas Combuchen
Kent Hunter
Hans Neubert
Rike Sethiadi
Johan Vipper
Kin Yuen

Earl Gee Design
501 Second Street, Suite 700
San Francisco, CA 94107

Tim Girvin Design, Inc.
1601 Second Avenue, 5th Floor
Seattle, WA 98101

Carin Goldberg Design
One University Plaza
New York, NY 10003

Pat Gorman Design
5 East 17th Street
New York, NY 10003
Pat Gorman
Frank Olinsky

Handcraftedfonts Company
P.O. Box 14013
Philadelphia, PA 19122
Jonathan Macagba

Harp and Company
2970 Olcott Road
Big Flats, NY 14814
Douglas G. Harp
Susan C. Harp
Linda E. Wagner

Hello Studio
285 West Broadway
New York, NY 10013
Helene Silverman

Hill/A Marketing Design Group, Inc.
3512 Lake Street
Houston, TX 77098
Jeff Davis
Chris Hill
David Lerch

The Hoefler Type Foundry, Inc.
611 Broadway, Room 840
New York, NY 10012-2608
Jonathan Hoefler

H²N Design
1468 West 9th Street, #630
Cleveland, OH 44113
Peter Nguyen

Mirko Ilic
652 Hudson Street, #3W
New York, NY 10014

Alexander Isley Design
361 Broadway, Suite 111
New York, NY 10013

Mac James
594 Broadway, Suite 1215
Box 1201
New York, NY 10012

KINETIK Communication Graphics
1615 17th Street, Northwest 2nd Floor
Washington, DC 20009
Jeff Fabien

Lisa Levin Design
124 Locust Avenue
Mill Valley, CA 94941

Manhattan Design
See Pat Gorman Design

Randall Martin Design
5 Weehawken, #4A
New York, NY 10014

Stephanie Mauer Design
269 West 72nd Street, #10C
New York, NY 10023

M Plus M Incorporated
17 Cornelia Street
New York, NY 10014
Takaaki Matsumoto
Michael McGinn

MTV Networks/Nickelodeon
1515 Broadway
New York, NY 10036
Michelle Willems

Dennis Ortiz-Lopez Co.
267 West 70th Street, #2-C
New York, NY 10023

Our Designs Inc.
27 West 20th Street, Suite 400
New York, NY 10011
Natasha Lessnik
Randy Tibbott

Pantheon
201 East 50th Street
New York, NY 10022
Archie Ferguson

Pavement, Inc.
9360 Cole Drive
Stockton, CA 95212
Stephen Malkmus

Bennett Peji Design
5145 Rebel Road
San Diego, CA 92117

Daniel Pelavin
80 Varick Street
New York, NY 10013

Penguin USA
375 Hudson Street
New York, NY 10014
Paul Buckley
Michale Ian Kaye

Pentagram
212 Fifth Avenue
New York, NY 10010
Ron Louie
Paula Scher

Peterson & Company
2200 North Lamar, Suite 310
Dallas, TX 75202
Scott Ray

Petro Graphic Design Associates
315 Falmouth Drive
Rocky River, OH 44116
Nancy Petro

Portfolio Center
125 Bennett Street
Atlanta, GA 30309
Roger Richards

Random House Inc.
201 East 50th Street
New York, NY 10022
Archie Ferguson

RCA Records
1540 Broadway
New York, NY 10036
Jackie Murphy

Reverb
5514 Wilshire Boulevard, #900
Los Angeles, CA 90036
Andrea Fella
Somi Kim
Whitney Lowe
Lisa Nugent
Lorraine Wild

Richardson or Richardson
1301 East Bethany
Phoenix, AZ 85014
Neill Fox
Forrest Richardson
Valerie Richardson

Rigsby Design, Inc.
5650 Kirby Drive, #20
Houston, TX 77005
Lana Rigsby

Rolling Stone
1290 6th Avenue
New York, NY 10104
Gail Anderson
Debra Bishop
Angela Skouras
Fred Woodward

Jonathon Rosen
408 2nd Street, #3
Brooklyn, NY 11215

Rosenworld
54 West 21st Street, Suite 705
New York, NY 10010
Laurie Rosenwald

Mark Ryden Illustration
221 West Maple
Monrovia, CA 91016

San Francisco Focus
2601 Mariposa
San Francisco, CA 94110-1400
Matthew Drace

Studio Seireeni
708 South Orange Grove Avenue
Los Angeles, CA 90036
Romane Cameron

Simon & Schuster
1230 Avenue of the Americas
New York, NY 10020
Frank Metz

Smokebomb Studio
106 Norman Avenue, #122
Brooklyn, NY 11222
Brian Kelly
Nancy Mazzei

Spot Design
775 6th Avenue
New York, NY 10001
Drew Bodges
Peter Mackey
Vincent Sainato

Summerford Design, Inc.
2706 Fairmount
Dallas, TX 75201
Jack Summerford

THIRST
855 West Blackhawk
Chicago, IL 60622
Gib Marquardt
Rick Valicenti

30Sixty Design, Inc.
2801 Cahuenga Boulevard, West
Los Angeles, CA 90068

Twelve Point Rule
27 West 20th Street, Suite 904
New York, NY 10011
Henry Vizcarra

Robert Valentine Inc.
17 Vestry Street, 2nd Floor
New York, NY 10013

Jon Valk Graphic Design
245 East 24th Street
New York, NY 10010

Vintage Books
201 East 50th Street
New York, NY 10022
Susan Mitchell

The Wall Street Journal
200 Liberty Street
New York, NY 10281
Greg Leeds

Words + Pictures
3711 Glendale Terrace
Minneapolis, MN 55410
P. Scott Makela

Henry Sene Yee Design
526 Jersey Avenue
Jersey City, NJ 07302

Bruce Yelaska Design
1546 Grant Avenue
San Francisco, CA 94133

Index

Art Directors/Designers/Design Firms

Abelson, Danny 71
Allen, Terry 155
Anderson, Charles S. 120, 122, 181
Anderson, Gail 21, 48, 69, 91, 98, 129, 184
Anderson, Robert Clyde 156
Appleton, Robert 19, 63, 73
ArtRock 145

Baker, Richard 76
Balkind, Aubrey 29, 34
Bartholomay, Lucy 155, 183
Bates, Richard 74
Becker, Charlie 41, 57
Becker, Syndi 47
Benton, Ashlie 163
Bishop, Debra 21, 52, 100, 114, 150, 154, 164
BlackDog 43, 128, 156
Black, Roger 182
Bloch, Anthony 47
Boyd, Steve 41
Bricker, Thomas 66
Brown, Hugh 121
Buckley, Paul 162, 175
Burdick, Anne 37
Bustamante, Gerald 51
Byrne, David 135

Cabarga, Leslie 81, 106
Cameron, Romane 125
Campiz, Miriam 118, 119
Carson, Carol Devine 96, 99, 100, 166, 175
Carson, David 28, 31, 35
Castle, Jason 108
Chantry, Art 33, 40, 52, 58, 73, 114, 124, 128, 140, 141, 143, 147, 161, 169, 177
Chase, Margo 30
Chermayeff & Geismar, Inc. 68
Chocolate USA 56
Christensen, Jeff 117
Chung, Fani 100
Cohen, Marc 58
Combuchen, Andreas 29, 34
Comitini, Peter 132, 134, 157, 182
Cooper, Philip 144
Corning Corporate Design 184
Cosimini, Gary 88

Cowles, David 19
Cozza, Marc 47
Crolick, Sue 133, 154, 180
Cronin, Jean 63
Crumb, R. 168
Cuddy, Diane 119
Cuomo, Yolanda 21, 36, 146

Davis, Jeff 101
de Wilde, Barbara 100, 166, 170, 176
Deck, Barry 77, 105
Drace, Matthew 16, 25, 53

Earls, Elliott 80
Eiseman, Sara 24, 86

Fabian, Jeff 150, 174
Fanning, Lee Ellen 76
Fella, Andrea 75
Ferguson, Archie 16, 22, 87, 99, 166, 167, 176
Fey, Jeff 156
Fili, Louise 42, 53, 101, 113, 115, 155, 165
Fontana, John 167, 169
Fox, Mark 43, 128, 156
Frolick, Stuart I. 33
Frankfurt Gips Balkind 91, 92, 129
Frankfurt Balkind Partners 34, 66, 71

Gallentine, Todd 142
Gargiulo, Frank 23, 67, 75, 164, 177
Gee, Earl 18, 87, 91, 100, 114, 163, 171
Gilmore-Barnes, Catherine 136
Girvin, Tim 86
Gold, Jeff 87
Goldberg, Carin 16, 24, 42, 46, 56, 60, 86, 97, 101, 112, 116, 117, 119, 121, 160, 164, 165, 166, 167, 171
Gorman, Pat 52, 63, 130, 157, 168
Gotfryd, Alex 166
Gulick, Jane 140

Hamilton, Robert 163
Harp, Douglas G. 128, 131, 184
Harp, Susan C. 128, 131
Hatch Show Print 120
Hauswirth, Todd 122
Heine, Frank 104
Heustis, Estay 113
Hill, Chris 101
Hodges, Drew 115
Hoefler, Jonathan 83, 107, 115, 123
Holston, Stacey 168

Hunter, Kent 34, 66, 71, 29
Hurwitz, Bob 97, 112

Ilic, Mirko 88, 89, 160
Isley, Alexander 71, 132, 136, 137, 152, 170

Jay, John 86
Jaramillo, Raquel 165

Kane, Jean 150
Kaye, Michael Ian 156, 177
Kelly, Brian 30, 31, 35, 40, 53, 109, 144, 177
Kidd, Chip 19, 22, 40, 58, 59, 92, 96, 99, 115, 170, 175
Kim, Somi 41, 71, 180
Knowlton, Alexander 136, 137
Koserin, Linda 56
Kowalewski, Lynn 142
Kozik, Frank 144, 145
Kruger, Barbara 183

Latham, Laura 174
Lee, S. Sung 74
Leeds, Greg 46, 93, 119, 121
Lerch, David 153
Lessnik, Natasha 152
Levin, Lisa 163
Lewerke, Ria 42, 118
Licko, Zuzana 104
Loeser, Judith 113
Louie, Ron 22, 90, 117, 131, 162
Lowe, Whitney 77
Lynch, Robin 66, 87, 135

Macagba, Jonathan 106
Mackey, Peter 115
Maisner, Bernard 49, 50, 93
Makela, P. Scott 30, 32, 36, 68, 76, 177
Malabrigo, Mark 125
Malkmus, Stephen 56, 57
Manhattan Design 130
Marquardt, Gib 70
Marko 53
Marquez, Henry 119
Martin, Randall 47, 113
Matsumoto, Takaaki 151, 155
Mauer, Stephanie 128
Mayne, Thom 75
Mazzei, Nancy 30, 31, 35, 40, 53, 109, 144, 174, 177
McGinn, Michael 151, 155
Mendez, Rebeca 33, 160

189

Metz, Frank 46, 60, 101, 117, 119, 121, 165
Mitchell, Susan 58
Morphosis 75
Murphy, Jackie 42, 76, 118

Neubert, Hans 34
Newlyn, Miles 104
Nguyen, Peter 91, 92, 129
Nissen, Melanie 164
Norcross, Debra 177
Nugent, Lisa 17, 32, 72, 180

O'Grady, Tom 43
Olinsky, Frank 130
Olson, Daniel 120, 122, 181
Ortiz-Lopez, Dennis 82, 109

Pavement, Inc. 56, 57
Peji, Bennett 154
Bennett Peji Design 154
Pelavin, Daniel 116
Petro, Nancy Bero 81

Ray, Scott 50, 153
Reep, Sam 88, 89
Reverb 17, 32, 71, 72, 75, 77, 180
Richardson, Forrest 130
Richardson, Valerie 130
Richards, Roger 142
Rigsby, Lana 153
Robert Appleton 19
Rosen, Jonathon 62
Rosenwald, Laurie 51, 60, 169
Rosenworld 169
Rubinstein, Rhonda 182
Ryden, Mark 50

Sainato, Vincent 134
Scarlett, Nora 93
Schaap, Inge 63
Schaefer, Cathy 68
Scharff, David 140
Scher, Paula 22, 23, 25, 90, 117, 131, 150, 154, 162
Schuckhart, Kay 71
Seow, Jackie 130
Sethiadi, Rike 66
Shelton, Sam 150, 174
Silverman, Helene 24, 66, 67, 73, 75, 114, 117, 162
Skalski, Krystyna 16, 160, 164, 165
Skouras, Angela 118, 157, 176

Smith, Sean 42, 76, 118
Smokebomb Studio 30, 31, 35, 40, 53, 109, 144, 174, 177, 174,
Sokolow, Rena 17
Steele, Tommy 156
Studio Seireeni 125
Summerford, Jack 134, 135, 185
Swanlund, Gail 37

THIRST 34, 46, 151
Tibbott, Randy 152
Twelve Point Rule 140
Tylevich, Alex 32

Robert Valentine Inc. 61
Valicenti, Rick 46, 70, 151
Valk, Jon 129, 130
Vanderlands, Rudy 36, 37, 43, 77, 161
Vipper, Johan 29, 66, 113
Vizcarra, Henry 113

Wagner, Linda E. 131
Wagner, Lisa 56
Weaver, Victor 42, 112, 167
Wild, Lorraine 75
Willems, Michelle 48, 125, 131
Wilson, Julie 48
Winegrad, Naomi 36
Wold, Lorraine 75
Woodward, Fred 21, 47, 48, 51, 52, 69, 91, 98, 100, 114, 129, 150, 164, 176

Yee, Henry Sene 118, 132, 157, 167, 169
Yelaska, Bruce 97, 135
Yuen, Kin 20, 71

Illustrators

Allen, Terry 91, 155
Anderson, Charles S. 122
Arce, Alejandro 89
Avila, Roderigo 163

Barry, Lynda 168
Becker, Charlie 57
Blitt, Barry 16
Bramhall, William 46
Bull, Fran 146
Burns, Charles 115
Bustamante, Gerald 51

Carroll, Larry 35
Carroll, Tim 53
Castro, Peter 113
Clark, Tim 125
Clerc, Serge 169
Comitini, Peter 132, 157
Cooper, Philip 144
Cotton, Jay 75
Cowles, David 19
Crumb, R. 168
Crumb, Robert 143

Dahlk, Randall 122, 181
Derveaux, Isabelle 60
Drescher, Henrik 20, 63

Falls, Mark 87
Fisher, Chris 19
Flewellen, Neil 165
Fox, Mark 43, 128, 156
Francois, Andre 120
Friske, Maria 19

Gee, Earl 18
Greif, Gene 119
Gurman, David 46

Hartland, Jessie 61
Hirschfeld, Al 21
Holtgreve, Alfons 120

Igarashi, Takenobu 120

James, Mac 74

Kahn, Eric 77
Kelly, Brian 40

190

Lessnik, Natasha 152

Maisner, Bernard 49
Mak, Kam 137
Marten, Ruth 89
Mazzei, Nancy 40

Nessim, Barbara 112

Ortiz-Lopez, Dennis 91

Panter, Gary 75
Parks, Melanie Marder 167
Peck, Everett 176

Russo, Anthony 121

Skwish, A. 19
Steadman, Ralph 120
Steed, Ruth 117
Suter, David 93

Taborda, Philipe 120
Trenc, Milan 88

Valk, Jon 129
Vesalius, Andreas 184

Wernli, Ralph 132
Wiggins, Mick 119
Wray, Wendy 121

Letterers

Anderson, Gail 48
Bloch, Anthony 47
Brown, Calef 28
Carnase, Tom 46
Carroll, Tim 25, 53
de Camps, Craig 53
Derveaux, Isabelle 60
Fox, Mark 43, 156
Fox, Neill 130
Gee, Earl 163, 171
Gregg, Bill 129
Hamilton, Robert 163
Karl, Anita 21, 46, 47, 52, 98, 100, 114, 150
Maisner, Bernard 49, 50, 93
Olinsky, Frank 52
Ortiz-Lopez, Dennis 129, 184
Petro, Nancy Bero 81
Richardson, Forrest 130

Rosenwald, Laurie 51
Valk, Jon 129, 130
Yee, Henry Sene 169

Photographers

Adams, A. Patrick 124
Arnet, Angela 58

Bank, Kenneth 156
Becker, Charlie 41
Bell, Colin 28
Bland, James 58
Brewer, Art 31

Callis, Steve 32, 72

Dugdale, John 24

Eccles, Andrew 21

Frampton, Jerald 177
Friedman, Benno 16, 24

Gibson, Ralph 177
Ginsbergh, Alan 162
Gray, Todd 74
Guip, Amy 164, 177

Harp, Douglas G. 131
Heller, Steven A. 33
Hollyman, Tom 19
Horner, Michael 16
Humphrey Studio 119

Kasterine, Dmitri 19
Katzenstein, David 48, 99
Kern, Geof 174
Kidd, Chip 22
Klassen, Tony 70
Klein, Diana 23, 166
Komdelka, Josef 42

Larsen, Kristine 162
Leibovitz, Annie 66
Liberatore, Virginia 52
Lindgren, Scott, "Coop" 124

Mahurin, Matt 35, 98
Marcus, Barry 165
Marcus, Kurt 114, 166
Mc Glynn, Katherine 167
McGrath, Maryellen 118

Nelson, Geoffrey 100, 163, 171
Nugent, Lisa 32

Peardon, Lisa 63
Peterson, Charles 124
Plachy, Sylvia 21
Pleak, Drew 40
Pokress, Dave 183

Ritts, Herb 176
Roberts, Sharon 17
Rosa, Doug 164
Rosenberg, Merlyn 30, 142

Scarlett, Nora 93
Schuitema, Paul 100
Sednaoui, Stephan 87
Seliger, Mark 51, 52, 69
Shaw, P. Ollern 167
Skid 28
Spear, Geoff 176

Turner, Sheila 47
Turyn, Anne 22

Valicento, Rick 43

Ward, Keith 47
Watson, Albert 47, 98
Weber, Bruce 48

Ziolek, Lewis 157

A C K N O W L E D G M E N T S

The authors are indebted to Irene Vandervoort for providing invaluable research assistance. Thanks to Alex Isley and David Albertson for a splendid design that makes this book a wonderful toy as well as an excellent document. We are also grateful to the folks at PBC International; Mark Serchuck and Penny Sibal for inviting us to do this project; Susan Kapsis, our editor, another invaluable collaborator; Debra Harding for prodigious editorial assistance; Richard Liu, Garrett Shuh and Lorine Bamberg for their support and technical expertise. Without them this book would have been impossible. And finally, thanks to all the designers who showed us their playful sides.